CULTURE SHOCK!
Spain

Marie Louise Graff

Graphic Arts Center Publishing Company
Portland, Oregon

In the same series

Australia	India	Pakistan
Borneo	Indonesia	Philippines
Britain	Israel	Singapore
Burma	Japan	South Africa
Canada	Korea	Sri Lanka
China	Malaysia	Thailand
France	Nepal	USA

Forthcoming

Hong Kong
Italy
Norway
Taiwan

Illustrations by TRIGG
Cover photographs by Emma Lee (Life File)
Photographs from Life File Photographic Library

© 1993 Times Editions Pte Ltd
Reprinted 1994

This book is published by special
arrangement with Times Editions Pte Ltd
International Standard Book Number 1-55868-106-X
Library of Congress Catalog Number 92-81938
Graphic Arts Center Publishing Company
P.O. Box 10306 • Portland, Oregon 97210 • (503) 226-2402

Printed in Singapore

CONTENTS

ACKNOWLEDGEMENTS

So many people have been so very helpful that to try and list everyone by name would fill the book before it got started. I would, however, like to thank all those who were kind enough to complete my questionnaire and mail it back to me. Some of the responses have been incorporated in the chapter *Learning from Experience*.

Writing this book proved to be a fascinating experience! However well you may think you know the country you live in, you find you learn a surprising amount of new 'facts' when it comes to writing a book about it. However, any attempts at generalizing about the culture of a country must begin with a disclaimer ... no matter how much research may have gone into it, the result cannot avoid being coloured by the views and attitudes of the author.

My husband and I visited Spain originally in 1953 and have been living on the Costa Blanca, off and on, since 1973. All five members of our family agree that choosing to retire in Spain was perhaps the best thing we ever did. Without determined encouragement from my daughter Josie, I wouldn't have dared tackle the project but she kept insisting 'You can do it, Ma!' and jollied me along when I wavered. My grateful thanks for her perseverance.

Although every effort has been made to ensure that the information included is accurate and up-to-date, readers should be aware that rapid changes are expected during the course of 1992, when Spain becomes a full member of the European Community.

Marie Louise Graff
July 1992

5

INTRODUCTION

Any foreigner living in Spain will, to a certain degree, always remain a foreigner. You may have adapted beautifully to living in Spain, yet the Spanish culture will always remain different. This difference stems from the history of the country, the background to all the people who are 'Spanish' and 'Spaniards'. A foreigner may become Spanish by nationality, may even think and act like a Spaniard, but will never be a Spaniard at heart.

No land in Europe, possibly no land in the Western world, has such a forceful personality, such a strong flavour as Spain, nor such a proud history. This history not only forms the basis for the customs and traditions enriching the daily lives of the Spanish people, but also helps to explain their characters and mannerisms.

If you make little or no attempt to understand this history, you will remain just another foreigner living in Spain and will have little patience with the 'differences' you may encounter. If you make the effort to read a little about the country and its people and learn some Spanish, your experience in Spain will be enriched, and any possible culture shock may not be so traumatic.

If you are observant, you will soon learn to interpret the behaviour of a Spaniard, and as a consequence know how you should behave yourself. Manners are extremely important. Spaniards, although proud, are by nature polite and courteous. They are usually kind to foreigners. You do not need to imitate *how* a Spaniard eats to be accepted, but it is advisable to eat *when* he does. Demanding an evening meal at six o'clock may encounter resistance, and you should not expect Spaniards to accept an invitation if you insist on keeping to meal times with which they are unfamiliar.

'When in Spain, do as the Spaniards do' should be your motto – within the boundaries of common sense, of course. No need to abandon your own standards and culture in order to become Spanish. You are an *extranjero* (foreigner) and will remain an *extranjero*, but 'correct behaviour' will be appreciated and, if it does not earn you total acceptance, it will at least ensure cooperative friendliness.

Some expatriates arrive, settle down and remain. Others arrive, cannot settle and go away, taking all their grievances and prejudices with them. They are usually those who make no effort to understand the Spanish mentality but try to impose their own standards of behaviour on the people they encounter. Instead of trying to rush things, they should learn to relax. Spaniards tend to concentrate on enjoying the 'here and now' and letting 'tomorrow' take care of itself.

Tourism has changed the face of Spain for ever. Small fishing towns have expanded into cosmopolitan centres with large tourist hotels, marinas, skyscrapers and sprawling housing developments. Spain tends to become 'tourist' Spain, with 'pop' flamenco, second-rate bullfights and mass-produced souvenirs. The tourist can survive without having to eat Spanish food, drink Spanish wine, read Spanish newspapers or even try to speak Spanish.

Yet travel only a few kilometres inland and you will discover villages, towns, even cities, hardly touched by the coastal transformation. Unlike many places on the coast, they retain much of their traditional way of life, dignity and values, an admirable degree of cultural integrity, each place maintaining its own individuality. Much of Spain is like this, in fact.

In Spanish towns and villages untouched by tourism, the relationship between people and the land is a very close one. Agriculture is still very important: women work in the local fruit and vegetable packing factories, and most families grow crops. Family life is paramount. The tradition for parents to provide homes for sons when they marry means that many of the original small houses have been extended upwards or outwards to fulfil this commitment.

This is the Spain we want you to discover, not that of tourist brochures and travel magazines. The purpose of this book is to introduce you to Spain, its customs and traditions, its history and its people. You will experience a certain amount of culture shock, but armed with a little foresight and understanding, you will find it easier to accept your new surroundings and be accepted. Your enjoyment of Spain and the Spanish will thus be enhanced.

Chapter One

HISTORY AND DEVELOPMENT

One of the largest countries in Europe, Spain offers not only a wide variety of climates and landscapes but also a fascinating mixture of people with different cultural backgrounds. No one area nor any one Spaniard can be said to be 'typically Spanish'.

WHAT ARE YOU?

If asked 'What are you?' most people will answer 'I am English or American or French ...' and then proceed to specify 'I come from Devon or Florida or Normandy ...' ending up with 'My home town is Exeter or Miami or Cherbourg ...' The Spaniard, on the other hand, will reverse this order and start with 'I am from Denia' (most important), 'I am Valencian' (of secondary interest) and, if pressed further, will admit 'Oh yes, I am Spanish.' The Spaniard's individualism is reflected in this peculiar identification with the local area rather than the country as a whole. Such an attitude could be a result of the pronounced differences between the regions.

Anyone coming from outside Spain is an *extranjero* but even a Spaniard from the next village will be referred to as a *forastero* (stranger). To this day, Spaniards retain this extreme individualism.

In order to understand and appreciate Spain and its complexities, you need to know a bit about the upheavals that the country has suffered throughout history.

EARLY TIMES

Little is known of the original inhabitants of the Iberian peninsula. They were, however, responsible for one of the most famous examples of cave paintings in the world, the 'Sistine Chapel of the Neolithic Age' at Altamira. By around 2000 BC, the Phoenicians, then the Greeks, established trading colonies on Spain's Mediterranean shores. They came in search of silver, lead, copper and tin, and founded flourishing trading counters.

The Roman Invasion

After the Greeks came the Romans who became masters of all Iberia during the first century BC. By the second half of the third century, they had founded sizeable Christian communities whose social, cultural and juridical structures were well developed. The Iberian colonies thrived in the Roman Empire, producing three Roman emperors and several distinguished literary figures such as the Senecas, Martial and Lucan. The Roman influence is evident in the Romance languages spoken by the people: Castilian, Catalan and Gallego are all derived from Latin. The Romans have also left some outstanding physical evidence of their presence. Segovia's aqueduct and the

11

Great builders of infrastructure, the Romans left behind many vestiges of their stay in Spain: aqueducts, fortifications, amphitheatres, etc. dot the Spanish countryside. Some aqueducts are still in working condition today.

theatre and other ruins at Merida in Extremadura are imposing examples of Roman remains.

The Germans

Germanic invaders swept down Europe in the early part of the 5th century and ran over the Roman settlements. The Visigoths established the first unified kingdom about a hundred years later. However, the leaders adopted a Roman style of government and converted to the Catholic faith. Thus the Roman civilization survived three centuries of Germanic rule until the arrival of the Moors.

THE MIDDLE AGES

Arab invasions from northern Africa in AD 711 produced a new society which combined three distinct ethnic and religious groups. Christians and Jews, who had lived side by side for several centuries, were now joined by Muslims. Their mutual tolerance and collaboration led to an extremely rich culture resulting in such architectural masterpieces as the Grand Mosque in Cordoba, the Giralda in Seville and the Alhambra in Granada. The latter is probably one of the few 'wonders of the world' in which you might want to live. The Generalife, with its famous gardens, is less well kept but its atmosphere is well re-created musically by Manuel de Falla's *Nights in the Gardens of Spain.*

Moors and Christians

The Moors established their caliphate in the south but their power stretched to every corner of the peninsula. However, Christian kingdoms flourished in the far north and were eventually responsible for the rebellion which became known as the Reconquest. It took Christian troops seven centuries to achieve a definite end to Muslim rule in Spain, a triumph which continues to be celebrated to this day during the fiesta known throughout Spain simply as 'Moors and Christians'.

13

COLONIAL PERIOD

When Granada was taken back in 1492, the entire peninsula became unified under Ferdinand and Isabella (known as the Catholic Kings) and something that began to look like the Spain we know emerged for the first time. An Italian, Peter Martyr, who lived during the reign of the Catholic Kings, wrote: 'Who would have believed that the Galician, the fierce Asturian and the rude inhabitants of the Pyrenees, men accustomed to deeds of atrocious violence, and to brawl and battle on the lightest occasions at home, should mingle amicably, not only with one another, but with the Toledans, the La Manchans, and the wily and jealous Andalusians; all living together in harmonious subordination to authority, like members of one family.'

Expulsion of Moors and Jews

Unifying Spain was one of the greatest achievements of the Catholic Kings. However, the expulsion of the cultured Moors and the rich and industrious Jews left great gaps in the agricultural and administrative expertise of Spain. The Moors had been mainly responsible for the intricate terraces and irrigation systems which had created the exotic gardens and fruitful fields and orchards we still marvel at, and the Jews had been highly placed in court circles as advisers. Without the Moors and the Jews, Spain suffered from a decline in agriculture and the judiciary.

Christopher Columbus

However, an enormous empire came into being soon after Christopher Columbus discovered America.

GOLDEN AGE

In 1519 Charles I became Holy Roman Emperor Charles V, marking the birth of the Habsburg dynasty. His accession to the throne also signalled the beginning of Spain's 'Golden Century'. During his reign, Cortés, Pizarro and the conquistadores won a whole continent.

Christopher Columbus points the way to the New World from Barcelona.

The New World provided untold wealth to Spain and culture flourished in the Spanish court and noble houses. The most advanced artistic schools of Europe were encouraged to visit Spain. They produced an architectural and artistic heritage hard to equal anywhere else in the world.

The Inquisition

Philip II, Charles's son, succeeded him in 1558. Alarmed by the spread of Protestantism, he increased the scope and ferocity of the Inquisition which imprisoned thousands of 'heretics'. Hundreds were burned at the stake during the frequent autos-da-fé. The Jews who had not been expelled and had 'converted' to Catholicism were often suspected of practising their former religion in secret and suffered violent punishments.

The Armada

Spanish harbours in the New World as well as international trade were constantly being harassed by English 'pirates'. This eventually led Philip to raise a powerful fleet to invade England. This venture ended in the defeat of the Great Armada in 1588. Philip spent the closing years of his life in monastic austerity at the huge Escorial he had planned and had constructed on the bleak windswept slopes of the Guadarrama.

17th-Century Painters

The 17th century was Spain's 'golden age' of painting. Devotional artists of different character flourished; for instance, the ascetic Francisco de Zurbarán, the gentle Bartolomé Esteban Murillo and the Greek immigrant known simply as El Greco. This century also produced the first of Spain's indigenous universal geniuses – Diego Rodriguez de Silva Velasquez. If you are interested not only in Spanish but also in European culture, the Velasquez rooms in the Prado in Madrid are a must.

SPAIN'S DECLINE

However, the vast but distant empire in the New World was too difficult to govern from Spain. In the 18th century, the Habsburg dynasty was replaced by the Bourbons, and by the 19th century the only remaining colonies were Cuba, Puerto Rico, the Philippines and some parts of Africa.

First Constitution

Liberal ideas had an early start in Spain: the country drew up its first constitution in 1812. Conservatives and Liberals, although fighting each other over the new ideologies spreading throughout Europe, made peace in order to rid themselves of Napoleonic troops. (Napoleon's brother Joseph was made king of Spain in 1808.) Once independence was achieved, however, they were at it again and the 19th century reflected the turmoil experienced elsewhere in Europe.

TWENTIETH CENTURY

At the end of the 19th century, Spain had lost most of its remaining colonies in a war with the United States. The country began to suffer from an identity crisis. Several generations had witnessed tremendous political changes with no stability in sight. The Second Republic was declared in 1931 but civil war broke out five years later.

Franco

General Franco of the Nationalist forces finally defeated the other factions and put down the rebellion. From his victory in 1939 till the mid-fifties, Spain became internationally isolated. The term 'dictator' brings to mind a ruthless, self-seeking personality, and most of Europe considered Franco to be just that. However, under his regime, law and order was restored and, when he died in 1975, many Spaniards mourned his passing. Foreigners who chose to settle in Spain in those days also benefited from a somewhat outdated constitution which gave them tremendous value for money, practically no

17

crime to fear, and a variety of lifestyles to choose from. After Franco's death, the crime rate increased dramatically and houses which previously had been left unlocked and untended for hours at a time, now had to be barred and bolted against intruders.

SPAIN TODAY

Because of its eventful history, Spanish society is very varied and interesting. Today's Spain now benefits from a stable government and its entrance into the European Economic Community in 1985 signalled its return to the mainstream of continental life.

Gypsies

You will see gypsies in most parts of Spain, but most frequently in the south. Perhaps because of their reputation for being able to cast an 'evil eye', they are avoided and most Spaniards are reluctant to get involved with them. Even when it is known that they are responsible for small burglaries, these misdemeanours are 'tolerated' by the rest of the community in order not to provoke retaliation.

Cave Dwellers

It may surprise you to discover that there are several places in Spain where people still live in caves. Not all gypsies are cave dwellers, nor are all cave dwellers gypsies. Some of the 'caves' contain as many rooms as a large villa and are very comfortably furnished. They are said to be warm in winter and cool in summer.

The Monarchy

Following Franco's death in 1975, Spain became a parliamentary monarchy. King Juan Carlos is a modest monarch who runs a modest household and pays income tax like everyone else. In February 1981 he managed to suppress a rebellion of army generals when Lieutenant Colonel Antonio Tejero Molina of the Guardia Civil walked into the Cortes (the Spanish parliament) brandishing a pistol. His firm and

You will see more gypsies in the south of Spain, mainly in Andalusia. Traditionally a nomadic people, they do not hold regular jobs and many of them turn to begging or petty thievery.

immediate appeal to the army to remain loyal to him as commander-in-chief proved that the new democracy was strong enough to withstand a military coup. When he appeared on television in his army uniform, the whole nation knew that they now had a leader who would take them confidently into the 21st century.

LIFESTYLES

For the purposes of this book, Spain can be divided into three basic regional areas: urban, rural and coastal. The coastal regions can be further divided into coastal/urban and coastal/rural. The contrast between these areas is very marked and they offer the widest imaginable range of lifestyles.

Urban

The cities reflect the province in which they are found and carry the same name as the province. Since there are 17 autonomous commu-

San Sebastian in the Basque province bears a close resemblance to the French Riviera.

nities in Spain, cities tend to have their own individual identity. For the foreigner looking for a city in which to reside, the choice is wide.

Barcelona in the industrial north, big and bustling and proudly Catalan, is full of ancient Gothic architectural treasures as well as modern buildings, well-stocked supermarkets, luxury shops and large department stores.

Seville in southernmost Andalusia is very different, with its strong Moorish influence. The old Jewish Quarter, the Barrio de Santa Cruz, with its whitewashed houses, patios and balconies full of flowers, cobbled squares and twisting alleys is beautifully preserved.

On the other hand, San Sebastian in the Basque country on the north Atlantic coast has none of the flamboyance of southern Spain. Laid out in a very modern way, it is now a seaside resort on par with Monte Carlo or Nice.

Rural

Even though there are many highly cosmopolitan cities in Spain, a large proportion of the Iberian peninsula is still very rural. Enormous tracts of interior are devoted to agriculture. Grains, olives and, of course, vineyards in the central part of the country are a major source of wealth. Here can be found tiny medieval villages operating quite possibly without running water, electricity and telephones. Plains bordering the Mediterranean are extremely fertile. Always green, they are famous for their orange and lemon groves. Almond orchards provide spectacular shows of pink and white blossoms in the early part of the year. Fields south of Valencia produce vast quantities of the round-grain rice favoured for paella. More recently, they have even started to produce the long-grain variety.

Coastal

The various *costas* (literally meaning 'coasts' or 'shores') originally consisted of small seaside fishing villages. Many of the villages during the past two decades have been developed at great cost into

21

Benidorm then and now. In 1959 (top), the beach was a deserted stretch of sand with rolling hills in the background and a sheer cliff dropping to the sea. Today (bottom), you can barely see the sand, and the hills have been levelled to make way for hotels and skyscrapers.

international resorts. There are six *costas* situated between the conservative Costa Brava north of Barcelona and the 'jet set' ambience of the Costa Del Sol in the south. Midway between these two, the Costa Blanca, popular with retired couples from all over the world, claims to have the 'best climate in all of Europe'.

Resorts

The rapid development along the Mediterranean coast, spurred on by the ever-increasing numbers of tourists flooding in during the summer months of July and August, has created a lifestyle of its own. Places like Benidorm, which were quiet beauty spots before the tourist boom, now cater to thousands of happy visitors during the season. Towering blocks of apartments overlook the two lovely sandy beaches barely visible under the blanket of humanity spread over them. Be warned! If 'Far from the Madding Crowd' is your ideal, avoid Benidorm. As a general rule, resorts are crowded with holiday makers from all over Europe.

THE BALEARICS

These islands are a combination of coastal/urban and coastal/rural. Halfway between France and Africa off Spain's Mediterranean coast, Majorca, Minorca, Ibiza and Formentera became an autonomous province in 1983, but in many ways they remain independent of one another. Castilian Spanish was replaced on each island by a local Catalan dialect. Sign posts and road signs are even more confusing here than elsewhere in Spain.

Majorca

By far the largest of the islands, Majorca has a reputation for cheap package tours. This, however, is mostly confined to coastal areas. Inland you will find deserted monasteries, small museums, bird sanctuaries, caves and charming villages, all relatively unspoilt and full of character.

Minorca

The surprising thing about Minorca is its 'Englishness', the result of its century of British rule. Prehistoric monuments dot the landscape but its Georgian-style buildings and small tidy fields make it quite different from the rest of Spain. The language itself is peppered with English words. Franco punished this republican island after the Civil War by restricting tourism, but this was in effect a bonus – no high-rise hotels!

Ibiza and Formentera

Transformed by tourism from a mainly peasant society into a wild anything-goes type of place, the principal resort of San Antonio is now looked upon as one of the noisiest and most brash on the Mediterranean. By way of contrast, peasant women in their simple country costumes can still be seen collecting almonds in their aprons or herding goats.

THE CANARY ISLANDS

Just north of the Tropic of Cancer and about 150 kilometres (100 miles) off the coast of West Africa, the Canary Islands is a group of seven islands offering warm and sunny climates throughout the year. It is never too hot as the Atlantic sea breezes help to temper the climate. The archipelago became one of the 17 autonomous regions of Spain in 1981. These islands range from the large resort developments on Tenerife and Gran Canarias to the tranquillity and seclusion on the tiny islands of Gomera and Hierro.

There are regular car ferries between the islands and a fast jetfoil service between Tenerife and Gran Canarias. Transport on the islands themselves is generally quite good. Inexpensive taxi services are quite plentiful with metered fares for short trips and 'bargaining' for special fares for longer journeys. Bus services, with reasonable fares, are available on most of the islands, with Tenerife and Gran Canarias offering special minibuses called 'waa waas'. However, transport on the smaller islands is more limited.

If you are looking for lots of sunshine, Lanzarote and Fuerteventura are most likely to supply it. Fuerteventura has tracts of soft white sand dunes stretching for miles, allowing a fair amount of privacy, making it popular with naturists. Tenerife, on the other hand, has small black-pebble beaches. Lanzarote is unique with its lunar landscape of volcanic 'badlands', strangely beautiful and now designated a National Park.

INTERNAL MIGRATION

Literally millions of Spaniards flooded the cities in the fifties and sixties, causing shanty towns to spring up in the surrounding wastelands. These were eventually replaced by high-rise apartments, some of which were partly subsidized by the government. However, there were never enough to cope with all the migrants, and most families lucky enough to acquire an apartment were more than willing to take in lodgers, usually relatives.

PACE OF LIFE

Pace of life varies according to where you live. Big businesses in the cities are run at the same pace as their counterparts elsewhere. However, even in cities, Spaniards by nature are disinclined to rush their personal affairs. In rural areas, this characteristic becomes even more apparent. Farmers still travel about in their old donkey carts though this charming sight is becoming rarer.

One of the first things a foreigner needs to learn is how to match the Spaniard's conception of time. This will be dealt with more fully in the following chapters.

TIMES HAVE CHANGED

From a landscape of scattered towns and isolated villages, connected by a poor network of inferior roads, Spain now has well-maintained *autopistas* (motorways with a toll charge) and national highways in all directions.

From a land of deep-rooted traditions and long-established customs where strictly conventional behaviour and refinements of etiquette were accorded what may seem exaggerated importance to foreigners, modern Spain and today's Spaniard now more closely resemble their European counterparts.

One can safely say that Spain has caught up with the rest of Europe in almost every way, including cost of living which once was one of its main attractions. Nowadays the only items substantially cheaper in Spain are things like cigarettes and local wines and spirits. In this connection it should be mentioned that Spaniards are still enthusiastic smokers and 'No Smoking' signs are few and far between. However, anti-smoking legislation in Spain is now possibly the toughest in Europe. A few years ago, teachers might share a packet of cigarettes with their older pupils but these days smoking is banned in many public places, including schools.

All these 'changes' will be dealt with in the following chapters.

FUTURE SHOCK

Spain is expected to become a full member of the European Community in 1992 and further changes in the present social and economic structures can be expected.

Chapter Two

FAMILY AND CUSTOMS

CATHOLIC INFLUENCES

For centuries, Spain has been a strongly Catholic country with the Church and priests playing a big part in the everyday life of the average citizen. Most Spaniards are baptized, married and buried by the Church. The Roman Catholic Church does not recognize divorce and prohibits the use of contraceptives. These restrictions have resulted in Spanish families being very large, with strong ties among siblings. Today, however, economic considerations together with the process of urbanization, tend to limit the size of families.

A family picture. The extended family is still very common in Spain and you will find households where several generations still live together.

EXTENDED FAMILIES

Perhaps because so many millions of Spaniards migrated from rural to urban areas in the fifties and sixties, extended families are the norm rather than the exception in Spain. At that time, accommodation was scarce and because family ties have always been strong, several generations quite often lived together, sharing one house or even one apartment. These 'extended families' still exist. In the old days they were very close-knit, spending weekends together, and usually sharing at least two meals together. These days the young people, although they may live at home till they are in their twenties or even thirties, spend more time out with their friends than at home with their families. Most young Spaniards live with their parents until they get married and set up their own homes.

Children

V.S. Pritchett described Spanish women as being passionate lovers of children and claimed that there was marriage and eight children in their eyes. This was true in the old days when birth control was frowned upon and Spanish families tended to be large. Contraception was illegal and the birth rate remained high until the mid-seventies when it fell dramatically. Modern couples (especially those in the cities) now realize the importance of family planning and have fewer children.

Spanish children have always been treated like little princes and princesses. More money is lavished on their little suits and beautiful dresses than on their parents' clothing. They are obviously loved and pampered, even overindulged sometimes.

This indulgence becomes evident in the way Spaniards quite happily accept the presence of tiny babies and small children in

restaurants, irrespective of the time of day or night. When you take your family to a restaurant, don't be surprised if the waiter whisks your little darling off into the kitchen to be admired by the rest of the staff.

Even the smallest village will have a park with facilities for children such as swings, slides and sandpits. If you have small children, find a park near where you live and make a point of taking your children to play there. You may find it hard-going trying to communicate with other parents at first, but your children will soon start chattering to other youngsters. This is one of the easiest ways of meeting people and making friends in Spain.

In a big city with no public park nearby, the same result can be achieved simply by taking your child (or even dog) for a walk ... you will soon meet Spaniards who are out walking with their child or dog and before long compliments and comparisons are being exchanged.

Spanish Surnames

Surnames can be extremely confusing due to the fact that the mother's name is added on to the full name, so that in effect the middle name is the surname. For example, should your name be John James Smith, Spaniards will assume that your surname is James and Smith simply your mother's surname. Listings in phone books should therefore be checked carefully or you could find yourself listed under one of your Christian names! Spanish women do not change their surnames when they get married.

MANNERS AND MANNERISMS

Mannerisms and social behaviour are both influenced by the Spanish temperament which, as has been mentioned before, is strongly individualistic. In a general way Spaniards are one of the most formally polite of all peoples. Remember this when you are making introductions. However, do not take offence if you are not introduced to all the people in a room or at your table ... it may merely be that your name is too difficult to pronounce correctly! In such cases, it is quite in order for you to introduce yourself.

Certain Formalities

When meeting a Spaniard for the first time, it is a good idea to be as formal as possible. You should introduce yourself in detail, tell him who you are, where you come from and what you are doing in Spain. In return, he will welcome you expansively and tell you to feel at home. Only after such formalities have been exchanged will casual and friendly conversation take place.

Forms of Address

When addressing a Spaniard, Señor (Mr), Señora (Mrs) or Señorita (Miss) should be prefixed to the surname of the person to whom you are speaking. On better acquaintance, you may use Don (male) or Doña (female) with the Christian name. Nowadays Christian names alone are quite acceptable amongst the younger generation. Incidentally, wedding rings are worn on the fourth finger of the right hand, rather than the fourth finger of the left hand. If you are in doubt about the status of a woman, a quick glance at her right hand should clarify whether to address her as Señora or Señorita.

Kissing

Expect a handshake when you are being introduced but do not be surprised if you get kissed on both cheeks when you leave a party or any social gathering. This is quite normal in Spain. Women will kiss the men and the other women, but men will only kiss women. A man may give another man a big hug; it is just an expression of friendly feeling, nothing more!

In this connection, a young American married to a Spaniard told me: 'It has become so natural to hug or kiss everyone and their mother-in-law; an old boyfriend from my student days and his new girlfriend; a neighbour's visiting brother; a business associate's wife

... that when I go home to California on holiday, the people there seem very standoffish, and I have to curb my impulse to pass out hugs and kisses freely.'

Sneezing

It may come as a bit of a shock to hear a loud 'Jesus' after you have sneezed but this is simply the Spanish equivalent of 'Bless you'. In Spain the name Jesus crops up almost as frequently as Jose or Jaime and is often included in the name of a village. Foreigners may find it strange to see a village with a signpost saying 'Jesus Pobre'.

Dropping In

Before telephones became more easily available, dropping in was the accepted way of communicating with one's friends. Nowadays, however, this form of socializing is becoming rarer. Late morning or early evening were the usual times when refreshments could be offered and accepted. Now that most homes have telephones, this habit of dropping in has become almost obsolete since it is a simple matter to pick up your phone and invite your friends to whatever entertainment you have in mind. Should you find it necessary to drop in, make sure you avoid the post-lunch period when many people still enjoy a siesta.

MEAL TIMES

It is of course important to remember that meal times in Spain are a good bit later than in most other countries ... the midday meal is seldom served before 2 pm and the evening meal before 9. Breakfasts used to be the 'continental' type, serving only coffee or chocolate with a small roll or bun.

Nowadays, however, influenced by the influx of foreigners, hotels will serve fruit juices, fruit and even boiled eggs, and some restaurants are willing to cater to people wanting to eat at earlier hours. However, you may find yourself eating in solitary splendour should you venture into a restaurant before the approved hour in areas where tourists are less common.

This topic is more fully discussed in Chapter Eight (*Food and Drink*).

Table Manners

Americans who eat with only their right hand, keeping their left hand in their lap, should remember not to do this in Spain. It is considered bad manners not to have both hands clearly visible at all times! Spaniards eat with their knives and forks in hand at all times. When eating out, except in very upmarket restaurants, one is expected to keep the same knife and fork for every course.

Spanish table manners decree that you should keep both hands clearly visible above the table at all times.

VISITING HOMES

Spaniards rarely entertain in their own homes, usually preferring to do so at a favourite restaurant. Should you be honoured with an invitation to a Spanish home for lunch or dinner, a small gift may be appropriate – chocolates, flowers or wine. When you have a meal in someone's home, you will find that the hosts will keep offering you 'a little more'. They will be very insistent and you should in fact accept a little more or they will think you don't like the food they are serving. It's a sort of game they play, but a fattening one!

Foreigners in Spain, on the other hand, often prefer to entertain their friends at home rather than in restaurants. You will find that your Swedish friends will nearly always arrive with a bunch of flowers from the garden or a prettily wrapped bottle of wine. Not so common amongst the British, except on 'special' occasions such as birthday or Christmas parties, you may find yourself receiving a small gift if your guest feels unable to return your hospitality within a reasonable period of time.

Children are usually welcome wherever you go and are almost always included in parties. However, if you are invited to a Spanish home for the first time for a specific meal, don't bring the children unless they are invited. Once the Spanish family knows you and your children, you will find your children will be included in most invitations.

BIRTHDAYS

Children have birthday parties arranged for them by their parents, quite lavish ones on occasion. They invite lots of little friends who arrive with presents, and the parents organize games and distribute cakes and drinks. For adults, however, it is the reverse. The birthday boy or girl is expected to invite his/her friends, co-workers or classmates out for a drink or meal to celebrate his/her birthday. It needn't be more than a get-together over a cup of coffee, or a drink, but if it's your birthday, you are the host.

DRESSING FOR THE OCCASION

Once again, you will find Spaniards tend to be more formal than most other nations. In hot weather, of course, the dress will be more casual than in the winter months, but strapless tops may not be appreciated even in the middle of a heat wave, nor collarless T-shirts for men. When visiting government departments or any office in general, it is advisable to dress correctly. A friend went to the customs office and found himself being ushered in to see the man in charge ahead of others sitting in the waiting room. As he was leaving he could not resist asking why he had received this preferential treatment since he had not made an appointment. The answer startled him: 'If these people do not have the courtesy to dress in a respectful manner, they can wait all day ...' The people considered to be disrespectfully dressed included a man wearing a pair of shorts rather than long

A suit and tie are appropriate for all occasions, even when riding a scooter.

trousers, and another wearing flip-flops instead of shoes.

In coastal resort areas, dress has become more and more casual. It is not unusual to find tourists wandering about in supermarkets wearing scanty bikinis. This behaviour, tolerated in some areas, is not recommended if you intend to become a resident, though.

You will soon be able to recognize a Spaniard at a glance because even when they are dressed 'informally' they are usually immaculately turned out. In cities like Madrid, the women are very clothes-conscious and fashion is of supreme importance. They will spend huge amounts of money buying dresses and accessories just to keep up with the latest trends.

EATING OUT

Having a meal out is one of the most popular forms of socializing. To Spaniards eating is not merely a matter of physical necessity but a real source of pleasure. Don't be surprised to see whole families gathered round a table with small children sitting in their mother's lap and elderly grandparents joining in the fun. Mentally or physically handicapped members of the clan are often included in such outings. You may see the ladies of the party grouped together at one end of the table and all the menfolk at the other. This is because until recently Spanish women rarely mixed with Spanish men socially.

EVENING PASEO

Visitors to Spain are sometimes surprised to find towns and villages which appear completely devoid of humans. However, when the magic hour of the evening *paseo* (stroll) arrives, you may well wonder where all the people spring from. In some towns, the *paseo* takes place in the main square. In some cities it could occur along an esplanade. At around seven o'clock in the evening, you will notice a few fresh-showered, well-dressed young women, chatting animatedly together (rarely with a man) and walking sedately in twos and threes. More and more people begin appearing, including children and grandparents and an informal parade round the square or up and down the Ramblas takes place.

The evening *paseo* is a time for leisurely politeness and mild flirtation. Although the girls are in effect 'displaying' themselves, they do so proudly and seldom allow their eyes to meet those of a man.

Tradition dictates that a certain amount of care is taken with one's dress: you would not be too popular if you chose to join a *paseo* coming straight from the beach. In the coolness of a summer evening, joining a *paseo* is a pleasant way of taking gentle exercise and working up an appetite for the evening meal. For the older generation of Spaniard this may well be the only form of 'exercise' they enjoy.

TORTURA DE LA GALANTERIA

Translated, this means 'the torture of compliments and attention'. Spanish men tend to be very vocal with women, even those they do

37

not know. Do not be offended if you hear loud comments as you walk by … they are usually complimentary, more or less the equivalent of the American 'wolf whistle'.

COURTSHIP

Very attentive during courtship, the Spanish male appears extremely romantic and willing to do practically anything to win the favour of his beloved. He wants to sweep the girl off her feet and carry her off to his 'castle', but once he has succeeded, the relationship is likely to change.

WEDDINGS

Big or small, Spanish weddings will normally include some form of meal and your wedding gift is expected to be worth more than the meal you will be offered. Five thousand pesetas per person would be considered adequate in Madrid, less in smaller towns and villages. All the usual wedding gifts, such as silver, linen, crystal, even kitchen appliances, are appropriate. Wedding lists exist in cities, larger urban communities and even in some of the smaller villages. If a wedding list has been made, you will be informed of the name of the shop handling it.

MARRIAGE

Beautiful church weddings are the climax of many a girl's existence and her moment of glory, but once she is installed in her 'castle' it may at times seem more like a prison. From being a pampered and spoilt *novia* (fiancée/bride), she soon becomes the hard-working housewife whose duties consist of producing and caring for babies, and generally taking care of house and home, husband and family. In the old days, the husband was treated like a king and his merest whim was catered to. He was served first at meal times and often left the table before the rest of the family had finished eating. He was never expected to lift a finger in the running of the house, but wandered off to spend time with his male cronies, drinking *carajillos* (coffee laced with brandy) and playing dominoes in some bar. To this day you will find groups of men gathering in bars for this purpose.

'Second-Class Citizens'

Foreign girls marrying Spaniards were often surprised at the change of attitude which rapidly took place after the wedding. Their doting *novios* (fiancés/grooms) suddenly reversed the pre-marriage roles and expected to be waited on hand and foot. In those days women in Spain were very definitely second-class citizens. They seldom aspired to being more than a housewife, and very few tackled advanced studies and careers in business or politics. This has of course changed radically in recent years, particularly in urban and coastal areas. Many married women now hold a regular job, for financial reasons or for self-fulfilment. Among younger couples, husbands help with the housework and also look after the children, just as in other developed countries.

Divorce

Divorces did not exist until recent times. Marriages were made to last a lifetime, and even to this day, a divorce takes at least two years to be finalized. You have to establish the fact that you have been living apart for two years if the separation was mutually agreed upon, or five years if it was not. Otherwise you have to start the proceedings by obtaining a legal separation and either partner is free to petition for divorce after one year has elapsed.

Attitudes Towards Sex and Morality

In modern-day Spain, objecting to sex is considered by some to be as taboo as condoning it was in the past. In the last 10 to 15 years, women's attitude to sex has changed dramatically. In the old days, they were brought up to play the piano and also to play second fiddle to their husbands, doing everything in their power to further his career. Nowadays many women prefer to have careers of their own and they have turned to professions such as medicine and law. This has made them more demanding, open and authentic in their behaviour. No longer is it 'wrong' to talk about sex with friends and family. No longer do women consider orgasm a sin and a sure way of becoming pregnant. A divorced woman was called a 'black duck' (the equivalent of a black sheep) and shunned by her family and friends. These days many Spaniards get divorced and no longer are they treated as pariahs.

Husbands were always (and still are) expected to be unfaithful but these days the wives are likely to be equally unfaithful!

Modesty is a thing of the past for many Spanish women but nearly all still place a tremendous importance on 'appearance'. Wherever you go, you will find that Spanish women are greatly concerned about being well dressed. More and more young women work outside their homes and spend their money on the latest fashions.

SENSE OF HONOUR

Although the word 'machismo' originated in Mexico, it is a product of Mexico's Spanish heritage. The 'macho' concept involves a code of moral values centred on a peculiar conception of honour – honour which can be lost either by one's own actions or those of one's relatives.

As a general rule, Spaniards will treat you with astonishing courtesy, but remember that family ties are very strong. Spanish men may treat their women as second-class citizens and expect unquestioning love and devotion, but in return they will protect their women totally and will spring to their defence if there is any question of their honour being insulted in any way. Young foreigners should be careful how they approach Spanish girls who may have unusually sensitive and aggressive brothers or boyfriends nearby. Knives have been known to flash if a Spaniard becomes provoked.

SENSE OF HUMOUR

Spaniards may take offence if you pass critical comments about their country or their customs. Even if you intend your remarks to be taken as a joke, be careful what you say, and to whom. The Guardia Civil used to wear those plastic-looking black triangular hats. A foreign friend asked one why his hat was such a funny shape, and was lucky that this particular Guardia had a sense of humour. He replied, with a twinkle in his eye, that the unusual design allowed him to relax leaning against a wall without his hat falling off!

Chapter Three

LANGUAGE

The language barrier can be a very real hurdle for foreigners in Spain. Approximately half the people you will come across in the coastal areas will speak some English or French but your attempts at Spanish will be genuinely appreciated. They won't make fun of your mistakes but do try to get your ear tuned to the way they pronounce their words. It is much more gratifying to be able to speak like the locals.

OFFICIAL LANGUAGES

Most foreigners learn Castilian (*Castellano*) which is the 'official' language used by the majority of the mass media and in official documents. Most Spaniards you will come into contact with speak and understand it. However, most regions have additional 'official' languages, often used in preference to Castilian. Foreigners can get utterly confused by these variations.

Regional Languages

Some autonomous communities have a language of their own. For instance, the language of the Basque provinces does not resemble any other language spoken in Spain. (The Basques call their region *Euskadi* and their language *Euskera*.) In Galicia, they speak *Gallego*. Catalan (and its various forms, including *Valenciana* and *Mallorquin*), which is spoken in the eastern regions, sometimes sounds more French than Spanish.

This medley of languages can be disconcerting to foreigners who have learned Castilian Spanish, more so because each regional language has different pronunciations and spellings. For instance, who would think that Javea and Xabia are one and the same place? Or that Donostia is the Basque name for San Sebastian? However, with frequent interaction, you will soon distinguish the differences between Castilian and the regional language spoken in your area.

CORRECT PRONUNCIATION

In Spanish, the letter 'j' is pronounced as 'h'. For example, you should say 'Huan' when calling someone whose name is Juan. 'H', when it appears in Spanish, is silent ('ablo' for *hablo*).

Although more and more Spaniards are coming into contact with foreigners, they sometimes seem to find it difficult to understand a foreign accent. Correct pronunciation goes a long way towards correct understanding. If you go into a tobacconist's and ask for Piper cigarettes, pronounced English-fashion, you will get a negative result. Even pronouncing it 'peeper' won't get you any further. You must emphasize the second syllable and roll the final 'r' before the tobacconist's face will light up with a smile of comprehension.

43

On the other hand, you will find him scowling at you if you ask for 'Burro' (donkey) instead of 'Duro' (Hard Pack). One tobacconist got very angry thinking he was being called a donkey for not understanding the original request.

You should remember that in Spanish every syllable in the word is pronounced. Stress placed on the right syllable will also make your attempts at speaking Spanish more easily understood.

POLITE SPEECH

Spaniards are more courteous and formal in their behaviour than most other nationalities, and the foreigner will receive more help and cooperation if he behaves in the same way. Although Spaniards are capable of infuriating behaviour – they can be rude, forget to answer letters, be late or totally ignore appointments – face to face they are usually very agreeable.

You may not always be greeted with more than a hard stare from certain officials, but in most instances you will be treated to a smile and a greeting which will vary according to the time of the day and the formality of the occasion.

Greetings

Encantado (Pleased to meet you) is a useful word to know. On informal occasions, *Buenas dias* (Good morning) and *Buenas tardes* (Good afternoon) while daylight lasts, and *Buenas noches* (Good night) after twilight may be shortened to *Buenas* alone. There are a number of ways of saying goodbye: *Buenos* is sometimes used when departing, but *Adios* is more correct. *Hasta la vista* implies 'See you again soon', equivalent to the American 'So long'.

Spaniards may greet total strangers when they enter a restaurant and wish the other diners *Que aproveche!* (Enjoy your meal!) to which *Usted gusta?* (Won't you join us?) used to be the formal response. Social etiquette demanded a refusal with the words *Muchismas gracias* (Many thanks), whether sincere or not. Nowadays though, this routine formality is rare, and a simple *Que aproveche* or *Buen provecho!* is enough.

Please and Thank You

When dealing with the locals, it is far better to err on the side of excessive politeness than to risk being ignored for lack of an expected *Por favor* (Please) or *Gracias* (Thank you).

Por favor can also be used to attract the attention of shop assistants who may happily continue to chat to one another while you stand at the counter waving the item you want to purchase under their noses. Saying 'Psst!' or whistling would not be appreciated. In fact, the shop assistant may continue talking just to 'punish' you for your bad manners.

CONVERSATION

It may surprise you to discover that there are not too many occasions when your hard-learned Spanish will be put to the test, except when you go shopping or have to deal with local tradesmen. This happens particularly in the coastal, more touristy areas, where the predominant local population consists chiefly of shopkeepers, fishermen and farmers. They are friendly and helpful but have little in common with the average foreigner. Should you be working in the coastal regions, you would certainly find Spaniards with whom you could socialize but most of the coastal communities divide roughly into national groups, based on linguistic preference. Should you choose to live in a rural area, you would find it much easier to be drawn into village life, and in such cases you would have ample opportunity to speak Spanish, and even pick up some local dialect.

Urban Spaniards in larger cities like Madrid or Barcelona are of course more likely to have common interests with foreigners and, in these circumstances, conversations and friendships can blossom quite rapidly. However these same Spaniards, when they take their holidays at one of the coastal resorts, hardly ever bother to involve themselves with the foreigners residing there, and this is understandable. They come for brief holidays, to relax with their own families and friends. Trying to sort out foreign residents from foreign tourists simply does not appeal to them. They will be superficially friendly towards all foreigners but do not expect to be received by them in their own homes with open arms.

TELEPHONE ETIQUETTE

Some foreigners are taken aback when they pick up the phone and *Digame!* or *Oiga!* is barked at them. Either of these words is used in place of the English 'Hello'. Literally the first means 'Tell me!' and the second 'Listen!' which, all considered, is perfectly logical. The person answering the phone will say *Digame!* and the caller will preface what he wants to say with *Oiga!*

Until quite recently, telephones were few and far between. In some areas, years might go by from the date of your original application and the final installation of an instrument. You might think that having a telephone installed and even a number allocated means success, but do not give your number out at this stage of the proceedings. It has often happened that the actual connection takes several more weeks to be finalized. During this time anyone ringing you will get a busy signal and imagine that you do nothing but chat endlessly on your newly-acquired telephone.

Local Calls

Public telephones can be tricky. So if you have to make a call, just go into any bar or cafe and the bartender will let you use the telephone on the counter for a metered charge. Ten pesetas is the minimum amount for a local call, and 50 pesetas for calls to other provinces, all of which have their own area codes.

International Calls

You can dial direct to most countries. The international code is 07, followed by the country code, the area code and number. Rather than using a pay or hotel telephone, a simpler and more economical method of making a long distance call is to go to the local telephone office and ask the operator to place it for you. You will be sent to a cubicle when the call is connected and charged according to the meter. Many international operators are multilingual, so if you need assistance with your connection, ask for an operator who speaks your language.

MAÑANA

This popular word is used frequently by Spaniards, but foreigners should know that there are several possible meanings. Literally 'tomorrow', it can also mean 'later' or even 'much later'. It is safe only to assume that it does not mean 'today'. This can become infuriating if you are waiting for the electrician or plumber who has assured you that he will come *'mañana'*. You wait at home all day, but no one comes.

This attitude is not a sign of dishonesty. Spanish courtesy decrees that a negative answer to your question 'When can you come?' is unacceptable. The electrician or plumber hates to disappoint you.

Perhaps he really does mean to try and squeeze a visit to your house into his already overcrowded schedule, but experience will show that you really cannot rely on his *mañana*. If you are used to punctuality, this attitude can be really frustrating. You sit at home waiting, day after day, and no one appears; so you get fed up and venture out. When you come home, you find a note saying the equivalent of 'We came! Where were you?'. Getting angry with the fellow in question is a waste of time. He will agree with everything you say, smile and tell you he'll come '*mañana – seguro*' (tomorrow for sure) only to repeat the whole cycle. You simply have to learn to be extremely patient and accepting. Anger or frustration will only give you ulcers, and giving way to such emotions will not endear you to the plumber or electrician in question.

An American who has lived in Spain for the past 20 years says, 'Getting things installed or fixed is a nightmare! Much patience is required. A reasonably good excuse for not getting to work is "I had to wait all day for the washing-machine repairman" and quite often the repairman either doesn't show up at all, or else rolls up at 6.30 pm just as you are about to go out to dinner.'

If you want to make your stay in Spain a success, the first thing to get used to is *mañana*. This attitude is a national trait and nothing you can do will change it.

LANGUAGE SCHOOLS

As there is an ever-increasing demand for multilingual workers in practically every sphere, language schools have flourished in many areas. In some places, the regional government provides language tuition for adults. Courses for foreigners are usually around four months long.

PUNCTUATION

You may come across some forms of Spanish punctuation which may appear strange. For instance, marks are printed upside down before and the correct way after an exclamation or question: *¿Donde esta ...?* (Where is ...?)

USEFUL WORDS AND PHRASES

Please	*Por favor*
Thank you (very much)	*(Muchas) Gracias*
You are welcome	*De nada*
Yes and No	*Sí y No*
The toilets	*Los servicios*
The bill	*La cuenta*
Do you speak English, French, German?	*¿Habla inglés, francés, alemán?*
I can't speak Spanish	*No hablo español*
I don't understand	*No comprendo/No entiendo*
I don't know	*No se*
Where is ...?	*¿Donde esta ...?*
Left and right	*La izquierda y la derecha*

Straight ahead	*Derecho*
Up and down	*Arriba y abajo*
Open and closed	*Abierto y cerrado*
What's up?	*¿Que pasa?*

BODY LANGUAGE

Most Continentals, Spaniards included, probably use more non-verbal communication than either the British or North Americans. Compared with the French, Spaniards on the whole appear more conservative and less prone to excessive facial expressions and hand gestures. They may wave their hands about in descriptive ways, emphasizing whatever they are saying, particularly if they think that you, the foreigner, cannot understand their speech. For instance, when they want you to look at something, they are quite likely to say '*Mirar!*' (Look!) and simultaneously point at their own eye and then at the object you are intended to look at or admire. They may 'kiss the air' and shrug their shoulders to indicate 'It is of no importance', and they may wag a finger in the air to indicate 'Don't do that!' However, amongst the older generations, Spaniards are still extremely self-contained and dignified. Displays of affection between the sexes in public, for instance, would be considered in very poor taste, apart of course from the kisses exchanged as greetings or farewells.

Handshakes are never prolonged and only used at first introductions, after which kissing becomes the accepted form of greeting and/or farewell.

– Chapter Four –

RELIGION AND HOLY WEEK

CHURCH AND STATE

The Roman Catholic Church has played an important part in Spain ever since the Christians ousted the Moors and Spain became unified under the Catholic Kings. During the Franco regime, other religions were driven underground and in a general way the Church still permeates the lives of most Spaniards today, especially in provincial towns. The number of Spaniards in holy orders is still high by any standards. Each village has its priest who is often treated like a member of the family. In some households, no fiesta would be complete without the priest presiding at the table.

Religious Freedom

Religious freedom became a constitutional right under King Juan Carlos. Contraceptives are now on open sale and, despite Church protest, even abortions are permitted in certain instances. Spain has now become a secular state although the influence of the Church is still very strong.

First Communion

This still plays a major role in the lives of most Spaniards. First Communion marks the reaffirmation of a Catholic's faith in the Church. Families will spend more on clothes and celebrations, and relatives will come from all over Spain more readily for a First Communion than for any other occasion, including weddings. If you are invited to a First Communion, a small gift of jewellery or of religious significance (medallion, rosary, etc.) may be presented to the child. You should behave with decorum as is called for on such an occasion.

First Communion celebrations can occur in quite unexpected places. We were once surprised to find about 100 people congregating at our normally deserted mountain *merendero* (small restaurant), quite off the beaten track. It soon became obvious that this was a First Communion celebration, jointly organized by the parents of five or six little girls, all wearing the most beautiful lacy long white dresses. There was singing and feasting ... the paella was prepared out of doors on a wood fire in a pan measuring more than a metre across with the ingredients and several kilos of rice being stirred around with spades instead of spoons!

Saints' Days

Religion in Spain is not just a Sunday affair. For instance a typical religious and social custom is to call people up on their saint's day and wish them a Happy Day. Saints' days are just as important, if not more so, than birthdays. Your saint's day is the feast day of the patron saint whose name you bear. Of course you have to have a computer-type memory to record all such important dates in order to comply with this custom! However, if you do remember to call up a friend or colleague on their saint's day, it will be most appreciated.

OPUS DEI

This is a reactionary society which has a large membership, not only in Spain, but throughout the world. Opus Dei, the Work of God, is a curious blend of copied or inherited ideas. In its secrecy, exclusivity and structure, it mirrors Freemasonry and in its encouragement of hard work it resembles Protestantism. Its aim is to help its members practise the Scriptures in their daily occupations. Perhaps Opus Dei is the result of the lack of any serious rival to Catholicism in Spain. Although founded as early as 1928, this organization had comparatively little success within Spain until 1982 when it was granted a personal prelature by Pope John Paul II. Members were no longer accountable to the local diocesan authorities and this encouraged a revival in the fortunes of this strange society. Opus Dei accepts non-Catholic, even non-Christian, workers.

SHRINES AND SANCTUARIES

What is beautiful to the Spaniard is sometimes seen as rather macabre by the foreigner who may not be used to statues or idols featuring congealed blood. Most of the well-known shrines throughout Spain are home to either a statue of the Virgin or some holy relic. Both the statue and the relic are treated with enormous reverence. The statues of the Virgin frequently have rooms full of beautiful dresses and cloaks, jewellery and ornaments, and their outfits will be changed regularly. These statues and holy relics are paraded with great ceremony once a year on the feast day of the saint. Shrines and sanctuaries are considered holy places and you should treat them with great respect, just like the Spaniards do.

Religious pictures made of tiles decorate the walls of many villages. The Virgin Mary is a favourite.

The Virgin Mary

Statues of the Virgin Mary abound throughout Spain and most have their shrines in great monasteries which are full of magnificent art treasures. Some of these statues were discovered under miraculous circumstances and are credited with inspiring exceptional bravery in the Christians during their battles against the Moors. The black-faced image of the Virgin known as 'La Morena' at Montserrat is very small and old and dark, quite unimpressive, and yet it can attract as many as 2000 pilgrims and visitors at any one time. There is enough room for them all at the monastery, in addition to the Benedictine monks who reside there.

Foreigners may find it strange that the Virgin Mary plays a bigger role in the religious observances of Spain than does Christ, and she is frequently represented weeping.

GIGANTES AND CABEZUDOS

In certain towns, *gigantes* (giants) and *cabezudos* (big heads) are worn and paraded during fiestas. These 'giants' and 'big heads' are

grotesque figures, some up to 16 feet in height, some only a little taller than a man. Most of the figures are terrifying; some are very old, having been kept by the townspeople for generations. In Pamplona, these huge images representing Moors and Normans visit the town hall, dance before the cathedral and pay their respects to their patron saint, San Fermin, on 7 July when bulls are let loose in the streets. The public joins in and casualties are sometimes fatal.

CHURCHES AND CATHEDRALS

Every village has at least one church, usually high on a hill and crowned with a cupola-shaped roof of brilliant tiles, blue for the most part. There are more magnificent cathedrals in Spain than anywhere else in the world, most of them brimming with treasures. Some of the most interesting churches and monasteries include the Cathedral at Seville, the Mezquita at Cordoba, the Convent of Las Duenas at Salamanca and the Temple Expiatiori de la Sagrada Familia at Barcelona. If the doors are unlocked, you can safely assume that you can enter. Make sure you are dressed appropriately (i.e. in formal clothes) before going in. Even if no service is actually in progress, there may be people inside at prayer. Respect them and keep your voice lowered. The church may be brimming with art treasures, but it is not a museum for you to gawk at and exclaim over.

Services

In areas with large foreign communities, church services are available in languages other than Spanish. Times and frequency of services are advertised on notice boards in front of the church.

Some churches have choirs and perhaps a guitar accompaniment, and the singing is exceptionally attractive. In fact several self-confessed normally non-church-going friends say they now make an effort to go to the local church on Sundays simply to hear the singing even if this entails sitting through lengthy sermons in a foreign language!

Going to church on Sunday morning is an integral part of Spanish lifestyle. Many churches in the towns are modern in architecture.

When attending a church service, choose your apparel with care. Men and women are not expected to wear shorts or scanty tops when visiting churches or other religious establishments. Although it used to be customary for women to cover their heads with a scarf or kerchief in church, this is no longer necessary except perhaps in small villages and in less 'sophisticated' areas. The safest bet for men are trousers and shirt, and for women, a demure dress.

Foreign communities are now allowed the use of local churches where they can hold services in denominations other than Catholic, with their own *padre* (priest). These communities may extend their activities to include such money-raising affairs as Christmas bazaars, partly to cover the cost of their *padre* and partly for donations to local deserving charities.

CHRISTMAS

Until recent times, Christmas was not celebrated with as much enthusiasm in Spain as in most other countries, the death and resurrection of Christ at Easter being far more important in Spanish observances than his birth. It used to be impossible to buy Christmas cards in Spain, and turkeys were unheard of, Spaniards preferring a leg of lamb. Father Christmas or San Nicolas, who brings toys for the children on Christmas Day, made his first appearance in Spain on a Kodak billboard in the late seventies. As with everything else, times have changed, and Christmas trees and cards and presents are now easily available in most areas.

NEW YEAR'S EVE

You may find yourself wondering what to do with the 12 grapes handed to you just before midnight on New Year's Eve. Spanish custom expects you to swallow one grape each time the clock strikes the midnight hour. If you manage to down them all at the correct moment, you have earned yourself good luck for the coming year. If no grapes are available, you may be given a handful of raisins for the same purpose. But be careful! Small dry raisins are even more difficult to swallow in quick succession than juicy grapes.

TWELFTH NIGHT

In some parts of Spain, 6 January, celebrated as the Three Kings, is the grand finale to all the Christmas and New Year festivities. The three young men chosen to portray the Three Kings consider it such an honour that they will happily go into debt to make the occasion a memorable one. Children are given their main presents on Twelfth Night rather than Christmas, and the Kings throw handfuls of sweets as they parade along the streets. The processions and parades of colourful floats and beautifully costumed attendants on this occasion are an impressive sight.

EASTER

As already mentioned, Christ's crucifixion and resurrection at Easter is treated with more pomp and ceremony than his birth on Christmas Day. Easter is a time for celebration because it marks the victory of good over evil.

Holy Week

The *Semana Santa* ceremonics are perhaps the most beautiful and moving of all spectacles, and religious fervour runs high.

Foreigners who come to witness these occasions should treat them with great respect. Although the processions and celebrations are spectacular, you should remember their religious content.

Magnificent celebrations are held during Holy Week throughout Spain, especially in Andalusia and in the monasteries of Guadalupe, Escorial and Montserrat. Toledo, Valladolid and Saragossa also celebrate Holy Week with splendour. These celebrations take the form of processions where 'penitents' wearing the distinctively coloured hooded robes of their particular *cofradias* (confraternity or brotherhood) will accompany a pair of sculptured groups, one depicting a scene from the Passion and the other a Mater Dolorosa decked out in jewelled and heavily embroidered vestments. Each of these *pasos* (mobile tableaux), some of which date from the 17th century, is carried on the shoulders of about 100 men chosen for their strength. In Seville, the *pasos* sail through the streets amid clouds of flowers and glittering candles. They are greeted by strident wavering cries of '*Saetas*', impromptu arrows of song of *gitano* (gypsy) or flamenco inspiration uttered by gypsies as certain statues pass in front of them. Each will pass through the great cathedral to be blessed before being returned to its chapel.

Blessing the House

If you live in a rural area, do not be surprised if the village priest comes a-calling during the week preceding Easter. It is still his custom to visit each and every household in the village to bless the house for the coming year and receive a 'token of appreciation'. The priest will bless some salt and sprinkle your doorstep with holy water and, in return, you are expected to add an egg or two to the basket he carries especially for this purpose. If the basket appears to be too full, a donation of a few pesetas is a very acceptable alternative. This is a charming custom and refusing entrance to the priest because you are not Catholic will only create tension in the village.

FUNERALS

By law a burial or cremation should not take place sooner than 24 hours after death. However, it is not customary in Spain to delay a funeral and it will usually take place as soon as possible unless it happens to fall on a fiesta or a Sunday. Crematoriums exist in the larger cities. Funeral insurance is available and recommended as the company, through the local undertaker, takes care of all the paper-work, arranges and pays for the church service, and supplies a coffin, hearse and two wreaths.

Traditionally the family keep watch by the coffin (at home or in the chapel) all night long and relatives and close family friends are expected to call and keep them company. The length of the visit depends on the closeness of the relationship. As Spaniards are generally demonstrative, tears may be shed and there might be loud wailing and crying amongst the more emotional. However, most Spanish funerals are dignified and solemn.

Cemeteries

These are usually few and set well away from the village houses, enclosed by high walls and surrounded by dark needle-thin cypress trees. Most communities do not bury their dead in the ground. The coffins are slotted into a wall built to house a certain number of coffins. One either buys a niche 'in perpetuity' in which case the coffin will remain in its place as long as any relative remains alive, or the niche is rented for a period of five years. If no further payment is made at the end of five years, the remains will be placed in a common grave. Some foreigners find this method of dealing with death somewhat callous. The Spanish attitude towards death is certainly extremely casual. The burial walls can be several feet high and, if your coffin is intended for one of the higher niches, it could be hoisted up by a rickety contraption to the right height and then shoved into its hole quite unceremoniously by a Spaniard unconcernedly puffing on his cigar.

All Saints' Day

Celebrated in many parts of Spain as 'the Day of the Dead', 1 November is an occasion when the whole family will try to go to the cemetery to pay their respects. It is not a particularly sad time. Food may be brought along and families may stay all day, enjoying the chance to get together with all their relatives and catch up on family news.

Chapter Five

FIESTAS AND FERIAS

Spaniards work hard, and they also set about their fiestas with unlimited enthusiasm. Fiestas in Spain are frequent, fun and famous for their fireworks. Spaniards are a happy people and any reason is reason enough for a fiesta. Chances are one is being celebrated somewhere in Spain every day of the year.

FIESTAS

'A feast or festivity, holy day or holiday' is the dictionary definition of 'fiesta'. This hardly conveys the variety of fiestas enjoyed by Spaniards. From the smallest family party gathering to celebrate a birthday, anniversary or First Communion to nationwide holidays such as the Feast Day of St Joseph, fiestas are a time for families and friends, a time for all to enjoy themselves, from tiny children to aged grandparents. Relatives and friends will return from all parts of Europe to join the celebration. Men, women and children put on their finest suits and prettiest dresses and go out to have some fun!

Fiestas normally include:

- Feasting when lavish meals are served with lots of wine and laughter.
- Various kinds of processions depending on the occasion: small children parading in regional costumes; young adults fancily dressed and equipped as Moors and Christians; large and spectacular floats carrying elaborate papier mâché figures or holy relics.
- Music supplied by a single guitar with everyone singing, or village bands parading with the processions, or castanets clattering as background to flamenco singing and dancing.
- Bullfights, bull running or bull baiting.
- *Fallas* (papier mâché effigies) and fireworks.

PARTICIPATION

Fiestas are for the people of the whole town or village. Almost everyone takes part. Some posts have been held by members of the same family for generations. The money for the celebrations comes from door-to-door collections or from various other sources – a surplus in the refuse collection account, for example!

When Spaniards celebrate a fiesta, they really celebrate. However, foreigners should remember that most fiestas have a religious origin and, despite the festive air, the occasion is also of religious importance. So don't behave as if it is a fun fair.

By nature, Spaniards are loud. They talk loudly, laugh loudly, sing loudly, so of course they will be very noisy during a fiesta. Even those participating in the parades and processions are likely to shout

Street dancing is a feature of fiestas. These two girls in traditional costume are taking part in the San Juan procession.

greetings to their friends and family along the way. The foreign visitor, however, should not do the same. Unless you are specifically invited to join in, remember you are only a spectator. Be sure not to get in the way of any parade or procession. If presents are being handed out, do not expect one as your due. Spaniards love children and sweets are often given out. The Three Kings throw handfuls of sweets to the crowds lining the roadside during their procession. Do not grab at them greedily, even if they land at your feet. It is better to pick them up and hand them to the nearest children. Although Spaniards are friendly and welcoming by nature, they may not like having you intrude in what they may consider to be specifically their event, so be discreet.

FALLAS

Some fiestas date back to very early days and have a pagan element about them. Coinciding with the summer solstice, the fire celebrations which take place nationally on the night of San Juan are a reminder of pre-Christian rites. The *fallas* of Valencia are of this type. Huge papier mâché sculptures, usually representing politicians and public figures, are displayed in the streets for a week. Some can be quite gruesome and even phallic. All are set alight at midnight to create enormous bonfires and the fireworks which follow are noisy, spectacular, and sometimes frightening to those unaccustomed to such entertainments!

MACHO MEN

Spaniards consider bull running a national sport; the young and not so young men of the village will tease and encourage bulls to chase them down the narrow streets to enhance their 'macho' image. Occasionally such bravado backfires and someone gets hurt, but quite often the only bulls available are bored and docile beasts used year after year and therefore quite disinclined to 'perform' as desired.

Papier mâché figures, depicting well-known personalities or folk heroes, are paraded in the streets before being set alight on the final night of the San Juan fiesta.

Bull Running

If you are not accustomed to village fiestas, beware! Your introduction could be a bull chasing you down a narrow street. Barricades are erected in order to keep the bulls confined. However, unwary strangers have been known to duck under or climb over them only to find themselves suddenly faced with charging bulls. To avoid what must seem almost certain mutilation, if not death, they may in desperation climb the nearest lamppost or dive through an open window, possibly landing in the lap of a beaming old Spaniard, watching such antics with amusement from the safety of his house.

Pamplona

The bulls which run in Pamplona during the July fiesta should not be teased by the unwary. These bulls are bred for courage, stamina and ferocity, primarily for the bullring. Only the young and very fit should risk running with them. Casualties occur each year and some have proved fatal.

Bull Baiting

Some ports have their bull running on docks which are barricaded at one end with seawalls providing suitable seating for spectators. This is really bull baiting as the beasts need to be encouraged. Firecrackers and tin cans are flung at the feet of the bored animal to make it charge after the youngster who jumps out of the way. With luck, the animal's momentum will carry it over the edge of the dock into the sea, much to the amusement of the spectators. You might not approve but the bulls appear to enjoy their swim and are carefully craned up out of the water onto the dock side.

Spaniards taking part in such a pastime most certainly do not consider it in the least cruel, so you would be wise to keep your own counsel if you do not like the spectacle.

Nowadays foreigners of both sexes are encouraged to join in the fun but pre-teenagers attempting to enter the enclosure are politely, but firmly, discouraged ... after all, this could be a dangerous game and accidents have been known to happen.

Bullfighting

Many foreigners consider this sport cruel and unfair to the bulls, in fact decidedly shocking. To Spaniards it is an art form comparable to ballet, combining courage and technique on the part of the bullfighter, and stamina and cunning on the part of the bull. Not recommended for sensitive souls with queasy stomachs, the pageantry and spectacle of the serious bullfights can be breathtakingly beautiful. *Aficionados* (fans) watching enthralled, although aroused and excited, do not resort to violence.

Occasionally, the tables are turned. One bull was seen charging into a ring with such energy that it jumped over the barricades into the tiers of seating. The *aficionados* sitting there had no option but to leap into the ring, leaving the bewildered bull to race around the seats! This, however, is very unusual and could only happen in one of the smaller provincial rings.

MOORS AND CHRISTIANS

Many villages commemorate the battles between the Christians and invading Arabs during the Reconquest of Spain. Mock battles are staged over a three-day period with one army wearing chain mail made of fabric to avoid being overcome by heat exhaustion. Otherwise their opponents dressed in togas would win too easily. The Christians take possession of the castle and the Moors counterattack the next day when the whole village becomes a battleground. On the final day the Banner of the Cross is victorious.

Participants are often seen in the village bars fortifying themselves for the next stage of the battle. A foreigner might be alarmed to see one army throwing their enemies bodily out of a bar amidst blood-curdling yells, but Spaniards love this type of fiesta. Whole families will turn out to watch the processions and bands, take part in the dancing in the streets, and see unsuspecting foreigners leap into the air when firecrackers explode at their feet.

THREE KINGS

The procession of the Three Kings takes place on Twelfth Night. It is a great honour to be chosen as one of the Three Kings, so great that one young man sold his flat in order to have sufficient funds to pay for the costumes and the entertainments which are an essential part of being selected as one of the Kings.

FERIA

'A fair or market', feria usually refers to a gathering for the sale and purchase of bulls and/or horses. The Spanish talent for enjoyment turns many ferias into fiestas and they draw similar crowds; parades and processions, singing and dancing create the same excitement.

Although many cities are famous for the beauty and splendour of their celebrations, the feria in Seville at Easter is perhaps the most memorable of all with its gathering of *gitanos* dressed in their traditional long flounced, brilliantly spotted dresses and Spanish nobility parading their fine horses.

A Word of Warning

The feria is a fairground in every sense of the word and foreigners should be warned about pickpockets and con men. To avoid a possibly unpleasant experience, leave your jewellery locked up at home and make sure your handbag is securely held. You should take the same precautions even when merely walking around the weekly village open-air markets. A few years ago, mugging and bag-snatching were unusual but nowadays one hears of daring snatches in broad daylight, particularly in areas where gypsies abound. Even when you think you are securely protected in your car with the windows shut, do not be complacent. Windows have been smashed and bags snatched from the laps of surprised passengers. On one occasion, the car was being driven slowly through Valencia, traffic being particularly heavy because it was a fiesta, when the back door was opened and a youth reached in and grabbed the handbag which was firmly jammed between the front seats. By the time the driver and his passenger had freed themselves from their seat belts, the youth was nowhere in sight.

It would be unjust to imply that gypsies are responsible for all burglaries. On the *costas* north of Andalusia, foreign summer visitors have been known to enter houses where windows are invitingly left open to snatch what cash may be lying about.

ENTERTAINMENT

In addition to fiestas and ferias, you can find the usual types of entertainment in the towns and villages of Spain.

Cinema

Quite a few of the larger cities in Spain have theatres which regularly show foreign films in the original language. You will find these listed in the local papers and marked 'V.O.' for Original Version.

Alternatively, once you have mastered enough Spanish to understand a conversation, you could try one of the local shows. Spanish films are usually of good quality (Spain has produced several world renowned directors and actors) and watching a Spanish film will help you polish up your language skills as well as give you an insight into different aspects of Spanish society.

The Arts

Madrid puts on major arts festivals during all four seasons. Events include world-class jazz, *salsa*, African music and rock. Film festivals and art exhibitions can be enjoyed at reasonable prices. The venues are quite often city parks or open-air amphitheatres.

English language performances are a rarity but you won't need to know Spanish to enjoy the traditional operettas called *zarzuelas*, a sort of bawdy comedy. Concerts of classical music are very popular and the Auditorio Nacional de Musica in Madrid regularly hosts major orchestras from around the world.

Catalans are great art lovers and Sunday morning concerts in the Palau de la Musica in Barcelona are a popular tradition. The Gran Teatro del Licou is a very fine opera house, considered second only to Milan's La Scala. The season runs from November to March but may occasionally be extended into spring. Compared to New York and London, the prices of tickets are very reasonable.

Flamenco

Without any doubt, Seville and Jerez are the capitals of flamenco. The former has three flamenco clubs, but these are patronized mostly by tourists rather than by locals. Although Catalans are not too fond of this purely Andalusian spectacle, there are one or two night spots in

Come on! Anyone can do a flamenco! You will find the most authentic flamenco dancers in Andalusia, especially in Seville.

Barcelona catering to tour groups, but these can be very expensive.

Flamenco, essentially the creation of Andalusian gypsies, has been shamelessly exploited by the tourist industry. Your best chance of seeing and hearing good flamenco is to go to one of the flamenco festivals which are held throughout Andalusia during the summer months. These festivals attract the finest performers but they never really get going till the early hours of the morning and quite often last until dawn.

Sevillanas

This type of music and dancing, stemming from the Canto Chico, is commonly confused with flamenco by foreigners. This music is a mixture of folk and pop, and is traditionally performed during ferias,

71

the spring parties known as Cruzes de Mayo, and the annual pilgrimage to the Virgin of the Rocio. On these occasions of endless singing, dancing and drinking, pleasure is pursued to a degree seldom matched anywhere else in Western society.

LATE HOURS

It can be a surprise to discover that most entertainments do not start till late at night and that you are not likely to get to bed much before dawn. This applies throughout Spain and at all times of the year, not only during fiestas. Stamina is required if you want to keep up with the celebrations. It is a curious fact that Spaniards can dance all night and work normally the following day. Perhaps the siesta is a habit which foreigners should adopt quickly if they intend to keep Spanish hours.

Chapter Six

BUREAUCRACY AND RED TAPE

North Europeans find Spanish bureaucracy a subject for instant conversation. They moan, they marvel, they are outraged. From a North European point of view, the system may appear inefficient, tied up in red tape and possibly corrupt. To a Latin American, however, Spain is efficient, honest and friendly.

The tourist will have little contact with officialdom. The potential worker or resident will have much. Problems can be overcome to a certain extent by paying a middle man to take care of the negotiations. To do it yourself, though, is more fun and puts you in touch with helpful and friendly Spaniards.

Spain, like other European countries, is in a state of change as it becomes fully integrated into the European Community. Rules for people from the EC and for those from outside can be different. Changes in the rules take time to work through and this may lead to problems; offices in different areas may be working to different instructions.

RESIDENCE REQUIREMENTS

Living in Spain does not necessarily mean you need to apply for permanent residence. The first thing to decide then is whether you actually want to become a resident as this will dictate how you proceed. Foreigners coming to retire rather than to work quite often choose to remain permanent tourists, for a variety of reasons.

Residencias

Residence permits are identity documents (with your picture and fingerprint) which non-Spanish residents of Spain are required to carry. The first one lasts two years. Subsequently you can renew your permit for a further five years. It is essential that you have your passport stamped with a visa by a Spanish consul before you leave your home country. This visa is only good for 90 days and, if you want to apply for *residencia*, you must do so before it expires.

Other requirements may include all or any of the following. As they vary from district to district, you would be well advised to go to the foreigners' department of the nearest Comisaria de la Policia Nacional and check out the list of requirements which is normally posted there.

(a) Evidence of belonging either to a private health scheme or entitlement to public health services.
(b) Certificate showing you have no criminal record in your home country.
(c) Certificate showing you have a certain amount of pesetas in your bank.

(d) Proof that you have somewhere to live.

(e) Certificate that you have registered your presence with your nearest consul.

(f) Four passport-size colour photographs.

Next step is to buy a *papel de estado* (stamped paper) at an *estanco* (state tobacconist) which you hand in with your application to the Comisario who will tell you what the fee is in your case. You will be given a *resguardo* (receipt) which you must guard carefully until your application for *residencia* is granted.

In some instances, in addition to (c) above (proof that you have imported a certain amount of money from abroad), you may also have to prove a monthly income of a certain number of pesetas. The amount varies according to where you live. At time of writing the basic requirement is:

- 100,000 pesetas per person in the Marbella area
- 70 to 80,000 pesetas per person in Alicante
- 50,000 pesetas per person in Elche
- 80,000 pesetas per couple in Denia.

Amounts obviously vary considerably, so choose your area carefully to make sure you can afford this requirement. Even so, there is no guarantee that the monthly requirement will remain the same indefinitely.

As a tourist, you can stay in Spain for three months at a time. If you apply for and are granted a *permanencia* (temporary residence), then you can stay for six months. As long as you go out of Spain, even if only for a day or so, the three-month periods can be repeated any number of times. However, if you overstay your three-month period by even one day you risk being held up at the airport or border and made to pay a fine. A friend of ours, due to fly out of Madrid on an emergency errand, found herself held up for this very reason. Her three months had expired and no amount of explanations or excuses made any difference. She missed her flight and was only allowed to continue on her way after her fine was paid.

There have been no dramatic changes with Spain becoming a full member of the European Community. For people from the EC wishing to retire and become residents in Spain, all the above requirements are still necessary. For American citizens, it is advisable to pay a visit to the consulate in person to ensure that the application was correctly completed and all the necessary documentation presented at the right time. However, EC members wishing to work in Spain need neither a special visa nor a work permit. They must, however, register with the local police on arrival at their destination and supply their current address.

PURCHASE AND SALE OF PROPERTIES

A property bought by a resident can be paid for with 'interior' pesetas and any capital gains will be included in your Spanish income tax return if you sell it when you leave the country. ('Interior' pesetas are those brought into Spain as part of the requirement for *residencia*. Used for purchasing properties, they can be re-exported when the property is eventually sold. However, rumour has it that this will soon no longer be the case.)

A tourist selling his property will be charged a maximum capital gains tax of 35% if he has owned his property for less than two years. The tax becomes less the longer the property has been owned.

Title Deeds

Buying a house in Spain should be a reasonably simple matter but a word of caution is necessary in this connection. Even when the purchase is handled through a lawyer, care must be taken to check through the *escritura* (title deed) very, very carefully.

Urbanizations

If the property you are considering is part of an urbanization, there is less risk of finding you have no right of way over the only access road to your piece of land. Some developers, however, having sold all the

Property prices in Spain are low compared with many other countries in Europe. Many foreigners own charming whitewashed villas on the costas.

houses on a particular urbanization, may conveniently 'forget' to complete the urbanization requirements. Roads may not be properly surfaced, or street lighting required by the municipality may not be installed, or perhaps your electricity has not been properly connected. There are endless possibilities along these lines and this is where the real test comes because trying to get such matters finalized can involve you in a great deal of running around.

Property Owners' Associations

There are usually associations in areas where most foreigners settle which specialize in assisting foreign property owners. Some of them publish monthly bulletins to keep foreigners up to date with any changes in Spanish laws which might affect them personally.

Multas

A *multa* is a fine. Some associations regularly publish the names of members who have in some way infringed a Spanish law. This is known as the 'early warning system' and has on occasion saved the owner from having to pay fines for non-payment of a tax about which he knew nothing. If he happens to owe a large amount in unpaid rates or taxes, his property could be put up for public auction in order to raise sufficient funds to pay the outstanding debt. This could happen without his knowledge, should he be out of Spain at the time. Owners have been known to return to find they no longer own their properties.

If you pay your *multa* in cash, you will be pleased to discover that you get a 20% discount!

SPANISH BUREAUCRACY

It is a fact that for many years Spain was very 'backward' in comparison to the rest of Europe. Spaniards were content to run things

on a very casual basis, not concerned that it might take a whole day to get a specific permit simply because it necessitated travelling all over the town or city to collect all the bits of paper and all the signatures required. Tremendous progress has been made in the last few years and efforts to streamline administrative offices have overcome some of the worst confusions and delays. But even to this day, your patience will be tried to the utmost on occasion, and you must learn to remain calm and reasonable under quite severe stress. Visits to official departments, notaries, etc. can involve much time and patience, not just for foreigners but also for Spaniards. They accept it as normal and often with humour. As one Spaniard once said, 'The delays are deliberate. This way one makes friends; you talk to people while you wait.'

ELECTRICITY

Electricity failures are much rarer nowadays except when there have been particularly savage storms or unusual amounts of snow. In recent years, electricity supply lines have been going underground but it is still quite common to see villages festooned with electricity lines from house to house and street to street. One wonders why more people aren't electrocuted!

If you find your electricity going off suddenly, first check your main fuse. If all your fuses are in order, the next step is to ring the electricity people. They may tell you that they are laying new lines and not to worry, your supply will be restored in an hour or two, or they may tell you that your bill hasn't been paid. This is normally taken care of by your bank, but mistakes can occur.

One couple we know, comfortably installed in their new house, delighted with the seeming ease with which they had 'settled in Spain', were surprised to find that their electricity supply seemed to be free of charge. They did not worry about it until the day they were warned it was about to be cut off. Then they found out that their small urbanization, a total of seven houses, had only one electricity meter

Although much progress has been made in the area of electricity supply, many village streets are still festooned with electricity wires.

in the name of the developer. He had been paying the account until he suddenly ran out of money.

Their immediate thought was: 'Fine, we can get our own meter.' But when they applied to the electricity board, they were informed that no meters could be allocated to individual houses on the estate until roads and street lights, etc. were completed to the standard required by the municipality. Since the developer was bankrupt, how to get this done? Of the seven houses, only three were more or less permanently occupied. The owners of the remaining four only used them for brief periods in summer and were therefore unlikely to want to fork out vast sums to finish roadworks and install street lamps. The short-term solution involved the three resident owners raising sufficient funds between them to pay the outstanding electricity account, which at least allowed them a period of approximately two months to figure a way out of their dilemma before the next bill was due.

Frequent meetings of the resident owners, including conferences with the local mayor and municipal architect and legal advisers, and numerous exchanges of letters with non-resident owners informing them of actions being taken and requesting their share of contributions for payment of bills led to the eventual discovery that no progress could be made unless the seven owners of the urbanization teamed up and created a 'community', for which purpose a special law exists to govern how owners should conduct their joint affairs.

Ley de Propriedad Horizontal

The law of horizontal property applies anywhere where owners possess things in common, such as pools, tennis courts, roads or sewage disposal systems, and in this particular instance ... the electricity meter! At time of writing, at least the owners know how to proceed but no one has dared predict how long it will take before the matter is finalized and each house supplied with a meter of its own.

Electrical Appliances

The electric current in Spain is 220 volts and the plugs take two round prongs. So, if you are coming from the United States, you will need an adaptor for things like hair dryers or other small appliances. I once thoughtlessly plugged in a hair dryer bought in the States and left it on my dressing table for a short period. I came back to find that my hair dryer had melted!

WATER SUPPLY

Before the influx of foreigners buying properties and building pools, the water supply along the coastal areas was adequate, apart from in the deserts around Murcia and Almeria. Then came the drought years when the rainfall was less than normal. Houses which had been built without *depositos* (holding tanks) to store water faced problems. Water cuts were frequent and restrictions on water usage quite stringent. The water-table in some areas dropped so low that sea-water penetrated the underground wells. Even if water came from the taps, it was often too salty to be used in cooking or for watering plants.

Fortunately this situation has been remedied by two years of adequate rainfall. The water in most areas is now of a sufficiently high quality for drinking and cooking, though many people still prefer to buy bottled water for personal consumption.

BASURAS

More or less efficient garbage collecting systems exist in most areas nowadays. If the circuit of the garbage lorries does not include your urbanization or area, there are large skips placed at frequent intervals along the roads into which you can dump your household refuse. Because of the pollution caused by random dumping of rubbish, some municipalities actually print a pamphlet specifying the correct procedures to be followed. Care must be taken not to scatter rubbish indiscriminately around the skips. You might find yourself pounced on by a *basura* (garbage) inspector lurking nearby and watching carefully to ensure correct use is made of the skips.

Street Cleaning

If you are accustomed to the streets being cleaned by municipal workmen, it may come as a shock that, in some villages and small towns, you are expected to keep the pavement, gutter and road outside your house clean. The proper way to do it is by sprinkling water from a bucket (a hard-to-master technique) or with a hose. In Spanish households, this task is still largely performed by women.

DENUNCIAS

These are oral or written complaints made to the local Guardia Civil, police or town hall about the action or inaction of a third party. For instance, if your handbag is snatched from you whilst you are browsing around an open-air market, you go along to the Guardia and make a *denuncia* to the duty officer who takes down the details on his typewriter. You will need a copy of this *denuncia* should you want to claim on your insurance.

If the dog next door keeps you awake all night or your neighbour scatters his *basura* carelessly on your drive, you could make *denuncias* but it is advisable to make them only about really important matters.

A *denuncia* permits the police to take action, but does not guarantee that you will get satisfaction.

TAXES

Residents are charged income tax on world income. They may also have to pay local taxes and sometimes a wealth tax as well. Property-owning tourists should pay the local property tax, the wealth tax and income tax on the letting value of their property in Spain even if the property is never rented out. You are deemed a fiscal resident if you remain in Spain for more than 183 days in a calendar year. You do not need to submit income tax returns if your yearly income does not exceed 900,000 pesetas (£5400 or US$9000).

CARS

While you are applying for *residencia*, you will be permitted to import a foreign registered car without paying customs duty. However, as soon as your *residencia* is granted, your car will have to be replaced with a Spanish-registered one. However, you do not need to do so if you have obtained a *prorogacion* (special exemption) before you applied for *residencia*. It may be granted for one year on payment of a proportion of import duty, and this can be repeated for four consecutive years, after which you either complete the importation or remove the car from Spain. As the customs valuation of your car may be higher than you anticipate, it is wise to get a quotation before committing yourself.

Although a large American or European make of car may be more comfortable for long-distance travel, it is as well to remember that many of the older towns and villages have very narrow streets which hamper the use of such cars because their wide beams make them difficult to manoeuvre.

Many villages in Spain date from the Middle Ages. Their narrow streets make large American cars very impractical.

Foreign Registered Cars

A tourist can use a foreign registered car for six months (nine if you are from 'overseas', i.e. USA, Australia or the Far East, etc.) per calendar year in Spain. If you want to leave your car in Spain but only spend six months of the year there personally, you can get the customs to 'seal' your car during your absence. However, the *prorogacion* procedure is also available and extensions can be obtained by temporary importation as mentioned above.

Car Papers

You are required by law to have 'car papers' with you whether you are driving a Spanish or foreign registered car, so that these can be presented to the police upon request. These papers include the registration book, insurance certificate, your own driving licence and personal identification papers. If you have a *residencia*, it is unlikely that your passport will be required. If you are caught driving without these papers, you might find yourself having to pay a hefty fine.

Driving Licences

As a resident with a Spanish registered car, you will eventually have to acquire a Spanish driving licence. To get one, you must apply to the Jefatura de Trafico in any provincial capital by presenting your licence and paying a small fee. After quite a lot of paper work and possibly an interval of some hours, a Spanish licence will be handed to you, but your original one will be retained. However, as a Spanish resident, you can use the Spanish licence anywhere in the EC.

International Driving Licences

If you are officially a tourist, it is advisable to have an international driving licence. However, a Spanish translation of your national licence is also acceptable.

WORK PERMITS

If you are coming from outside the EC and plan to reside and work in Spain, you have to apply for a work permit. This can take time to process, depending on the sort of work you plan to do. The ministry of labour has to be satisfied that you are not displacing or depriving a Spanish worker and the police have to be assured that you have no criminal record.

Self-employment

If you want to be self-employed, it may take you up to six months or more to get your project approved and licensed. However, you still need a work permit and other documents to work in your own business. (See Chapter Eleven for details of *Business and Working Conditions*.)

At time of writing, tourists are not allowed to work in Spain.

INSURANCE

It is advisable to have your house and contents insured and this is easily done through anyone of the many insurance companies, either

Spanish or foreign, operating in the towns and cities. They will probably send a representative to inspect your property and advise you about security measures. If you own paintings and/or other objects of particular value, it is best to itemize them or even have photographs available so that they can be more easily traced should they be stolen.

Your car must carry at least third party insurance and this too can be easily arranged locally.

Taking up life or medical insurance is a question of personal choice. If you have reciprocal national health benefits, registering with a doctor in your community will entitle you to free medical treatment and medicine. However, in some instances, additional medical insurance appears to be desirable, particularly in the larger, more crowded cities where private treatment would doubtless ensure speedier attention in times of emergency.

Chapter Seven

SETTLING IN AND ADAPTING

Lifestyles vary considerably depending on where you choose to reside. How quickly you settle in will depend on a number of factors, chief amongst which is the answer to 'How adaptable are you?'.

WEATHER CONDITIONS

One of the first considerations when deciding where to stay in Spain is what sort of climate you are looking for. Spain offers you a wide range to choose from. Basically a land of brilliant hot sunshine and cold black shade, Spanish landscapes and climates are anything but monotonous.

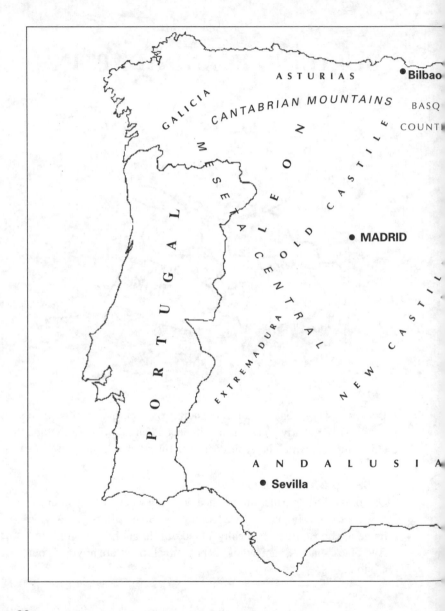

The 'Far North'

Galicia, in the northwest, is often likened to West Ireland, plentiful rainfall producing lush green hillsides and the half-submerged valleys called *rias*. Further along the coast, Asturias with its wild countryside and coal mines is more like South Wales. The pastoral farming and sound of cow bells in Cantabria next door could almost make you believe you were in Switzerland. The Basque country also presents an alpine aspect with farmhouses like Swiss chalets. During winter it rains almost continuously, producing a vegetation of an intense shade of green not to be found elsewhere in the country. The Pyrenees foothills are like Scottish Highlands, but if you go further south into Navarre, you will find vast stretches of tawny-golden undulating countryside around Pamplona and vast expanses of vineyards as you go even further south.

The Meseta

It may surprise a newcomer to discover that Spain, one of the largest and hottest countries in Europe, is also one of the highest. Apart from the Ebro and Guadalquivir valleys, the coastal plains rise sharply up to the Meseta, the vast central plateau which is approximately 2000 feet (600 metres) high and covers two-fifths of the peninsula. Here the bright light can hurt your eyes and temperatures soar in summer and plummet in winter. You can travel for miles and miles and never see a person or a village.

The Costas

Few people realize how cold it can become in winter, even on the *costas* which are famous for their long hours of sunshine. True, the sun does shine and, if you find a corner sheltered from the wind, you can sunbathe in your bikini in midwinter, but the moment you go indoors, you will probably have to don several layers of warm clothing. Few of the older houses have central heating. Most depend on wood-burning fires and portable gas heaters which provide pockets of warmth in otherwise icy atmospheres. Villas are often built with the intention of remaining cool in summer and, as a result, can be alarmingly draughty in winter. Even though you may not need a fur coat outdoors, thick sweaters can be useful indoors.

The Southeast

The countryside becomes drier and more mountainous the further south you go until you reach the desert/moon landscape around Almeria which was featured in spaghetti Westerns in the 1960s.

The Deep South

Andalusia comes closest to most foreigners' idea of Spain, perhaps because tourist promotion posters usually show a bullfighter in his fancy regalia, or a beautiful señorita in her spotted flamenco dress strumming a guitar. Such images are more readily found in the South.

The balmy climate all over Spain allows you to have a drink at an outdoor cafe even in winter.

The landscape is varied and powerful. The snow-capped Sierra Nevada range contains Spain's highest peaks. The great river Guadalquivir is surrounded by fertile pastures, marshlands and beaches. Stud farms and bull ranches abound. Here too there's brilliant sunshine and deep shadows.

The Muslims from North Africa occupied this area for nearly 800 years and left a deep impression, especially in architecture. Buildings are whitewashed to keep them cool. In the bright sunlight, the effect is simply dazzling.

Rainfall

Parts of Spain which are on the arid side may only have eight inches (203 mm) of rain a year but those eight inches may all fall in a single day. On the Costa Blanca this type of rainfall usually occurs towards the end of summer, and the first really big storm, accompanied by thunder and lightning and torrential rains, is called the *gota fria* (cold drop). Havoc quite often results because streets do not have drains or gutters and torrents of water will cascade down towards the sea, sweeping everything lying in their way. Flash floods can occur with surprising ease and cause serious damage.

'Sahara Rain'

You might be surprised one day to be caught in a rain shower and come home with either you or your car covered in muddy splashes. This does not mean that you carelessly drove through muddy pools; it means that the rainfall contained a fair portion of Sahara sand which, being pinkish in colour, stains everything it lands on, including your recently painted brilliant white villa and the tiles in your freshly cleaned pool. Your garden too will look as if it is suffering from some strange leprous disease. You may have to hire a high-pressure hose to remove the stains but you will be glad to know that this will not need to be done more than once or twice a year.

Summer Sunshine

Intense sunlight can age you prematurely and etch lines on your face unless you are very careful. Always use an effective sunscreen whenever you go out during the day. Rather than being pleasant and relaxing, the summer sun can be quite awesome, obliterating all activity and reducing you to a state of torpor. During the other seasons, however, the extra light and warmth can only be a bonus for people from less sunny climes.

DAY-TO-DAY LIVING

Some people claim that the coastal resort areas are not Spain because of the large numbers of foreigners residing or visiting there, and that if you choose a coastal area, you might just as well go elsewhere and be surrounded by your own compatriots. This is true up to a point but

Villages nestling on a hillside are a common sight in Spain. Conditions may be more primitive, but living in a village is a wonderful experience.

what you may not be able to find elsewhere is the combination of wonderful sunshine, beautiful scenery, an easy-going ambience and last but not least ... the Spaniards themselves.

Foreigners probably find the *costas* the easiest to settle in as they are geared to cater for non-Spaniards. You can find both rural and urban settlements on the *costas*. Rural villages can still be rather primitive and village folk suspicious of strangers, but if you adapt to their way of life, you will find them dignified, courteous and friendly. If you choose to live in one of the big cities, your day-to-day existence will of course be very different. Most city-dwellers are business people, and working conditions for foreigners in Spain will be dealt with in a later chapter.

City Transport

Madrid has an excellent metro system which is quick, frequent and cheap no matter how far you travel. Even cheaper is the 10-ride ticket called *billet de diez* which is accepted by the automatic turnstiles. City buses run from 6 am till midnight, both the red full size buses and the yellow microbuses which are somewhat more comfortable. Taxi stands are numerous and taxis are easily hailed in the street – except when it rains!

In Barcelona, the subway is the fastest and cheapest way of getting around as well as the easiest to use. Although a flat rate is charged no matter how far you travel, buying a *Targeta T2* is even more economical. Good for 10 rides, it is valid for metro, *tramvia blau*, funicular and central *ferrocariles* (railway). However, by buying a *Targeta T1*, you will also be entitled to travel on buses.

THE POSTAL SYSTEM

The Spanish postal system is seldom praised for speed and efficiency, particularly in the coastal areas where the influx of large numbers of foreigners has placed heavy demands on available postmen. The number of postmen in a certain area depends on the number of 'registered' residents in that area. If more foreigners registered with the local authorities, the situation would improve greatly.

Mail Deliveries

Letters are usually delivered once a day and to your door if your letter box is conveniently placed. Sometimes, in more rural areas, a number of boxes are grouped together at the end of a road so that the postman need make only one stop. Small parcels will be delivered to your door, but a larger one will be kept at the post office and you will receive a notice asking you to collect it. Proof of identity will be required.

A limited number of post office boxes are available in most post offices and these are allocated on a first-come-first-served basis. You may have to wait some time before one becomes available for you. However, letters addressed to you Poste Restante (called *Lista* in Spanish) can be collected on production of your passport.

SHOPPING

Cities and towns have department stores, boutiques and supermarkets where you can find the same items of daily use as elsewhere in Europe. If you live in a village, of course, you may have some difficulty getting smart clothes, furnishings and luxury goods.

In small towns and villages, most shops have no name or sign outside – everyone knows what they sell and where they are. The shopping is mostly left to women, although men may go to the baker's for bread. Women who are not working make shopping a daily affair, a social occasion, with separate trips to baker, supermarket, bank or butcher. Loyalty – often family loyalty – means patronizing the same shops, except on the days when the weekly open-air market is on.

Food shopping is a real treat in Spain. The range and quality of seasonal fruits and vegetables is excellent; dairy products tend to be more expensive than elsewhere in Europe; chickens are first class; and although Spanish butchers chop up meat in ways which you may find odd, once you figure it out, you can buy what you want.

The bakery is a regular stop for full-time housewives on their shopping rounds.

Metric System

It is useful to remember that Spaniards are unlikely to understand pounds and ounces. Should your request for 'a pound of potatoes' draw a blank look, rather than repeating your request, you could try pointing at the potatoes and asking for *medio kilo, por favor* (half a kilo, please). Some shopkeepers understand English.

In fact if you work on the basis that half a kilo is equivalent to one pound, you will be getting approximately the amount you desire. If you don't know the Spanish name for what you want, pointing at it is quite acceptable.

Covered Markets

Large or small depending on the size of the town or village, these markets are made up of rows of stalls, some selling fruits and

In a covered market, a butcher's stall advertises the sale of bull meat after a bullfight.

vegetables, others chickens and eggs, or meats and sausages, and some a variety of grocery items including cheese and other delicacies. One stall will be devoted to breads and cakes of all kinds, another may display containers full of pickled vegetables and masses of differently flavoured olives. These covered markets are still popular with local people even though they are in fact no cheaper than the big supermarkets which have sprung up everywhere.

Open-Air Markets

Each village has an open-air market once a week on a specific day when stalls are put up in neat rows offering the widest imaginable range of goods for sale. The vegetable stalls are a joy to behold, with their piles of red and green pimientos, stacks of huge shiny purple aubergines, mountains of enormous white cauliflowers, and boxes of luscious strawberries in season. Although salad items are available throughout the year, some vegetables are seasonal. If you buy 'seasonally' you will not be disappointed; the prices are lower. In general, locally grown vegetables and fruits are cheaper than in Northern Europe.

In addition to food, open-air markets usually have rows of stalls displaying clothing items, shoes, handbags and belts, as well as tourist items. But don't think you will be getting bargain prices. Check out prices in local shops offering similar goods and you will find the market prices are sometimes even higher, specially designed for the unwary tourist in a hurry.

Haggling

You will gain no advantage by bargaining with a stall holder over the price of potatoes or carrots because standard products in daily demand are sold at standard prices. However, if you are looking for items such

You can try your bargaining skills at a gypsy stall. But do not haggle if you have no intention of buying.

as watches or small radios, you might succeed in lowering the asking price. Also the carpet-sellers from North Africa and the gypsy women selling lace tablecloths may be willing to haggle.

Don't haggle just for the fun of it as stall holders will resent your wasting their time. Do haggle if you know the price you are prepared to pay and are keen to acquire the item in question. When the stall holder tells you his price, you make your offer. What this may be depends on what you are prepared to pay. You could start with a quarter of his asking price, with the intention of working up to half, or start with half and stick to it. When the final price is agreed, try to hand over the right amount of pesetas because if you give the seller a large note for a small amount, he may decide that you can afford to pay more and tell you that you misunderstood the agreed price.

Beware!

Pickpockets and bag-snatchers have a field day amongst the massed shoppers at open-air markets. If possible, you should leave your

handbag safely locked up at home, and clutch your purse or wallet tightly in your hand.

Hypermarkets

Most sizeable towns will have one of these enormous supermarkets where virtually everything under the sun is available. Here you will find the prices fractionally lower than in the smaller supermarkets. Some hypermarkets will even offer to repay *autopista* (highway) fees to encourage customers from outlying areas.

Department Stores

If you don't speak Spanish, these would probably be the easiest way for you to do your shopping. El Corte Ingles is a chain with a wide range of good quality items. Its main competitor is Galerias Preciados which can also be found in most of the major towns.

Queues

Spaniards do not like forming queues. Lining up one behind the other seems to go against their individualistic character. Consequently watch out for people trying to cut in. This *yo primero* (me first) trait also applies to driving in the city or on open roads, a case of 'survival of the fittest'.

Even though Spaniards do not form neat and orderly queues, they instinctively manage to keep good order and take their turn at the right time. Market stall holders will refuse to serve a 'queue jumper' and simply ignore him till they are ready to serve him. Nowadays, there is a system of numbers at some of the supermarket counters, particularly the butcher's. You take a number from a roll fixed on the counter and wait for it to be called. If there are lots of numbers ahead of your own, this leaves you free to carry on with other shopping till your turn draws near. But make sure you are available when your number is called. Otherwise you will be made to draw a new number and wait all over again.

Shopping Hours

Open-air markets start early and pack up soon after 1 pm; covered markets follow Spanish custom and are closed during the afternoon hours of siesta, but they do stay open till quite late in the evening, some as late as 9 pm. Supermarkets too observe the siesta and usually reopen only around 4.30 pm, although the family-run ones tend to have their own opening hours. As small grocery stores in villages tend to be both owned and run by a family, the hours kept can vary considerably. However, most of them would observe the siesta. Hypermarkets and department stores remain open all day.

SOCIALIZING

Spaniards love to gather together and talk, and you will see groups of old men sitting in bars, talking and playing cards or dominoes, or sitting in the village square, talking ...

Spaniards are a gregarious people. The women will gather on doorsteps to exchange the latest news and gossip, and family groups consisting of several generations can often be seen partying together. However, you may be surprised to find that Spaniards do most of their socializing out of doors, or else in bars and cafes. They very seldom entertain even their own friends in their homes.

Spanish Neighbours

If you live in an apartment block in one of the larger cities and have Spanish neighbours, you will probably become close friends in due course. But, if you live in an urbanization, it may be more difficult to make friends with the people occupying the other houses. However, in most instances, should there be any form of 'emergency', no matter how minor, your Spanish neighbour will leap at the opportunity to help in any way possible.

For example, should you suddenly develop a violent pain in your stomach and retire to your bed wondering how to get hold of a doctor, your wife need only mention your 'problem' to your Spanish neighbours. You will probably be overwhelmed with their 'attentions'. Not only will they send their son running to fetch a doctor, but they themselves are quite likely to wander into your bedroom to assess your condition, and offer sympathy in the form of a bottle of whiskey.

Spanish Houses

Homes are very private affairs in Spain. Unlike 'townhouses' found in other parts of the world which usually have a small front garden and a bit of a back yard, providing perfect opportunities for neighbours to exchange friendly chatter over their fences, a townhouse in Spain will have neither. A glance through the large and heavy front doors will usually be rewarded by the sight of attractive inner courtyards, full of greenery and pots of flowers and occasionally a fountain tinkling away. The home is the domain of the Spanish housewife who, whether working or not, diligently cares for home and family.

Older people like to meet in the park for a game of chess or dominoes.

Spaniards liven up their balconies with potted plants and bright flowers.

However, don't be surprised to find Spaniards gathering on the pavement in front of their houses to exchange the latest 'news' whilst enjoying the evening breeze in summer or the last rays of sunshine in winter. Foreigners are often puzzled by the Spanish preference for 'street socializing' rather than 'at home socializing'. This, however, encourages neighbours and local residents to get to know one another more intimately. You will find yourself being politely greeted should you stroll past such an outdoor gathering. Here's your chance to practise your Spanish by exchanging a few pleasantries!

Townhouses have become increasingly popular with foreigners as they offer far more security than villas set in gardens in an urbanization. They are also much more economical to maintain and easier to run.

Domestic Help

In the old days, many families could afford a string of servants and retainers. Nowadays most households are satisfied if they can have a cleaning woman come once or twice a week, and even these are becoming rarer now. The younger generation of Spanish women would far rather get a 'proper job' if they have enough education; even serving in a supermarket is far more appealing than cleaning someone else's silver.

However, it must be added that Spanish homes are immaculate. Housewives are extremely house-proud and devote themselves to maintaining a very high standard of cleanliness and tidiness.

Should you find yourself in an area where domestic help is available and are confronted by a Spanish woman eager to offer her services, one of the things you should make very clear right from the start is exactly what her duties will encompass. The pay is usually so many pesetas per hour and it would be wise to check around your suburb or village to find out what the local rate is. If you agree to pay more than the accepted local rate, you might find yourself very unpopular with the other residents!

Strangely enough, the sparkling cleanliness in the Spanish home is not duplicated in the streets. These tend to be littered with paper wrappers, cigarette butts and even discarded bits of food. An effort to improve this situation has caused numerous rubbish bins to appear in strategic places in most public areas. Even if the locals still throw their rubbish on the street, you should use the bins. Set a good example, and encourage the locals to improve the condition of their streets.

Joining Clubs

Some clubs are exceptionally expensive. A recent survey put Spain at the top of the list, the annual fee for a tennis club being the highest in Europe. Golf clubs and yacht clubs are all pricey to join, no doubt because their inability to expand due to lack of space may require them to limit their memberships. Some clubs are very exclusive and the typical Spanish reluctance to say no outright may raise your hopes of acceptance. Your name will be put on a waiting list but you may find yourself waiting indefinitely. However, if you do join a club, you will certainly find it a good way to meet Spaniards and other foreigners with interests similar to your own. Joining gardening societies or philatelic clubs can be achieved at almost no cost and there are amateur theatrical groups in most places.

Children have clubs which promote the same kind of community spirit as the boy scouts or girl guides. Most of the cities, towns and even villages have well-equipped parks, and there are zoos, amuse ment and safari parks to be visited. In Barcelona, Catalunya in Miniature comprises 72,000 square yards (60,000 square metres) of the province's most famous buildings, including the complete works of Gaudi, all scaled down, and the Parc Guell is a very popular playground for the city children.

Gardening

Gardeners are available, 'professional' Spaniards or 'amateur' for-eigners, but many people prefer to do their own gardening. This can

107

be an extremely rewarding pastime. But take this word of warning –
do not try and grow all kinds of exotic plants not usually found in your
area unless you are prepared for disappointments. It's safer to have a
garden full of local bushes and flowers which can cope with the local
weather conditions without too much attention, and indulge your
desire for exotics by keeping them in pots.

Pine Trees

If you are a keen gardener there are one or two things about pine trees
you should know. Pine trees can generate passionate support from
some people, and equally passionate hatred from others. When the
original vineyards covering certain parts of the coastal areas eventually died from old age, the terraces they occupied were in many cases
planted with pine trees, purely as a measure of soil conservation. The
resulting pine forests now cover enormous areas.

When we bought our *parcela* (plot) some 20 years ago the first
thing that had to be done was to get rid of enough pines (which at that
time were no more than 10 feet or 3 metres high) to make room for the
house. Romantic notions about pines dictated that a minimum number
of trees was cut down and this proved to be a big mistake. We soon
discovered that pine trees covering hillsides may look lovely and
green and conserve the soil, but pine trees growing in one's garden are
a different matter.

They not only drink all available water which makes them grow
at fantastic speed, but they shed thousands of needles with great
regularity, covering the ground so thickly that nothing ever grows
underneath their branches. Then there is the matter of pine pollen. The
first time we found our terraces and verandas covered in a thick yellow
powder, we were dismayed but not disheartened. However, we soon
discovered that sweeping up this yellow menace was a waste of time
as more would settle in the next few days. This lasts several weeks
early in the year. For people suffering from allergies, pine pollen can
become quite a problem.

But that's not all. Pine flowers start to fall and you find your garden covered in a brown carpet. Even this is not as bad as finding a caterpillar nest high up in the branches of one of your trees. These look like large footballs of dirty cotton wool and are unsightly in themselves. They are home to caterpillars with strange habits. When they leave the nest, they will travel in long lines, nose to tail. If disturbed they produce an irritant which can cause redness and swelling and which is extremely harmful around the eyes and mouth. Dogs which come into contact with these caterpillars can even go blind. The only way to rid yourself of the nests is by tying some cloth soaked in petrol to a long pole and then setting it and the nest on fire. A dangerous pastime, since pine trees are highly inflammable.

Forest Fires

In the past, most forest fires were accidental. But, in recent years there have been more deliberate fires, causing whole hillsides to flare up. Should there be a wind, the trees catch fire and explode into flame, and controlling such conflagrations becomes extremely hazardous. In the past few years, Spanish forests have suffered several damaging fires.

Never drop a cigarette butt out of your car window, and never leave a garden fire unattended.

Smoking

You can buy cigarettes and cigars from *estancos* (privately-run outlets for the state-controlled tobacco monopoly) at controlled prices. Some supermarkets also sell them, but at a higher price. You will find cigarette vending machines in some bars and public places but the prices will be higher.

Locally manufactured cigars and cigarettes are very cheap compared with other countries, which no doubt explains why Spaniards are still such heavy smokers.

I was once treated by a dentist who had a cigarette hanging from his mouth whilst he attended to me! Fortunately, this type of casual-

Most Spaniards do not heed the government's advice about smoking. Some of them still smoke whatever else they are doing.

ness is no longer found amongst the new generation of the medical and dental professions. In fact, anti-smoking legislation is tough and smoking is banned in most public places such as schools, hospitals and government offices where officials meet the public.

Drugs

Proximity with North Africa and links with Latin America make drugs like marijuana and cocaine comparatively easy to come by. A survey carried out some years ago on army conscripts showed that 60% had experimented with drugs by the time they enlisted in their late teens. Today it is difficult to find a young Spaniard who has not at one time or another smoked pot. The fact that it is not a punishable crime to be in possession of small amounts of marijuana for 'personal use' is certainly no deterrent. However, the real problem is in the trafficking of hard drugs which sprang up after Franco's death.

Madrid's airport, although it possesses some of the most sophisticated drug detection equipment in the world, still sees 60% of all South American cocaine passing through it, not only for the Spanish market but also for the rest of Europe. Many unemployed youths from all over Europe flock to the Balearics for a quick and cheap 'fix'.

MAKING FRIENDS

Having settled in the area of your choice and made efforts to adapt to your surroundings, will you now be able to make lots of friends? The answer is yes, but not perhaps as many Spanish friends as you might like. As already mentioned, the Spaniards are in fact a very private people, and for centuries women were kept at home and very much in the background. Even if you can speak Spanish and the local variety at that, you may find it disappointing that you are not welcomed into Spanish homes with open arms. Your friends may entertain you at a

Although Spaniards are a very home-proud people, they rarely invite friends home. Instead they prefer to meet you in a restaurant or cafe.

restaurant, they will be happy to play golf or tennis with you, or take you boating, but you will seldom be asked to enter their home. This is true of all the areas, although perhaps the urban Spaniard, being more sophisticated in many ways, is more likely to open his house to you.

What it boils down to in the end is 'How much effort are you prepared to make?' Unless you are willing to immerse yourself in the Spanish lifestyle, chances are you will eventually want to return to your home country.

On the other hand, 'I was lucky,' writes one American. 'I came at 20 with a friend. We ignored the "great American buffalo herd" and went off travelling and playing on our own. We adapted quickly. Within a month we'd been out with bullfighters and soldiers, doctors and clerks, and even home to meet some of their families and all of their friends. Spain is lots of fun if you make an effort to get to know the people.'

Most foreigners admit that although it may not be difficult to make friends, making 'close' friends is a different matter. 'Even though I speak Spanish fluently, there always seems to be some sort of barrier which impedes a close friendship,' says another American.

– Chapter Eight –

FOOD AND DRINK

Spaniards have a real reverence for food. A meal is an exercise of community spirit, for everyone gathered to enjoy the food and the company.

Spanish cuisine is as varied as Spanish landscapes and climates. Some palates may be offended by the generous use of olive oil and garlic in many Spanish dishes. But be adventurous. You will surely find something to suit your taste amongst the local dishes. Of course, these days there are lots of Continental (French, German, Belgian, etc.) and Eastern (Chinese, Indian, Indonesian, etc.) food available. Restaurants tend to provide a wide variety.

FOOD SHOPPING

Thanks to a mild climate and fertile soil, Spanish agricultural produce is cheap and plentiful making food shopping a real enjoyment.

Fresh Fruits and Vegetables

A wide range of natural produce gives variety and flavour to the cuisine of Spain. Spain being traditionally an agricultural country, one of the delights of Spanish cuisine is the excellent quality of the ingredients used. The wide geographic range results in the production of vegetables of all types which, for size, flavour and freshness, are hard to beat. Some, like sweet corn, were originally grown specifically for export because Spaniards thought of corn as cattle fodder. These days it is available in most supermarkets. Fruits include apples and strawberries, custard apples and persimmons, many types of grapes, citrus fruits and melons, just to name a few. All these are grown more 'naturally' than in most other countries. Spaniards insist on their produce being not just the freshest, but also as 'natural' as possible. Injecting oranges to improve colour and taste is unheard of in Spain. Spaniards prefer large lumpy half-green tomatoes for salads rather than the neat uniformly red ones (now also available) because the former have a far better flavour.

Convenience Foods

This is another aspect of Spanish eating habits. They prefer to eat fresh foods, bought and prepared each day rather than canned or convenience foods. Their diet, according to a recent medical report, is healthier than that of any other Western nation. If you come from a country where convenience foods are the norm, the range available in Spain is likely to disappoint you.

Gastronomic Delights

Spaniards will drive many miles to find a particular restaurant where a local speciality is being offered. Because some foreigners find it

Grapes galore at the weekly open-air market. All the fruits and vegetables in the markets are locally grown and you can get very good bargains.

difficult to adapt to Spain's idiosyncratic meal times, especially if they have children with them, it is assumed that they are unadventurous and have no interest in food. However, if you consider yourself a gourmet and are prepared to make some effort, you will not be disappointed. Outstanding food is more likely to be found in a village off the beaten track than in a luxury tourist restaurant. Restaurants which open before the traditional times tend to cater for the blander international taste.

EATING HABITS
Breakfast

Most Spaniards are satisfied with a breakfast consisting of coffee and a croissant, a roll or a small sponge bun. A fun alternative (but fattening!) is chocolate and *churros* – a portion of deep-fried dough sprinkled with sugar and dipped into a cup of thick hot cocoa. A great way to start the day!

Lunch

Usually considered the main meal of the day, lunch is eaten between 2 and 4 pm. In the city restaurants, you will have three courses starting with either vegetables, soup, salad, smoked fish or cured meat. Next will be a plate of meat or fish, and finally a dessert (*postre*) which can be a flan or ice cream, but most typically will be a piece of fresh fruit. Foreigners are sometimes surprised that the main course may be accompanied only by potatoes.

The lunch break being a lengthy one, most office workers go to a restaurant and have the *menu del dia* (set meal of the day).

Menu del Dia

By law, most Spanish restaurants are required to offer a *menu del dia* of three courses priced at 80% of what each course would cost separately. This *menu del dia* might be chalked up on a blackboard outside for all to see, or you might have to ask for it. In the latter case,

Churros *sprinkled with sugar are great with coffee or hot chocolate. They are very popular at open-air markets.*

117

it will probably offer the least appetizing choices to encourage you to order something fancier from the a la carte menu.

Dinner

Spaniards eat dinner quite late in the evening, at about 9 pm. This will consist of another three courses, sometimes with a lighter dish replacing the meat course. Nowadays most people find two such large meals too much and will replace one with snacks at a *tapas* bar or a sandwich at a fast food cafe.

Spanish Coffee

Spaniards drink their coffee very strong. It can be served in a variety of ways:
* *Café solo* is strong coffee in a small cup.
* *Café con leche* is coffee diluted with hot milk in a big cup.
* *Café cortado* is coffee diluted with milk in a small glass.
* *Café Americano* is not a special brew from America! It is a *café solo* diluted with water served in a big cup especially to suit the American palate. When ordering one, don't ask for an *Americano* without preceding it with *café* or you might earn yourself a very strange look from the waiter!

REGIONAL SPECIALITIES

All the regions have specialities of their own but paella is one which appears in a variety of forms in most parts of Spain. Consisting mainly of rice seasoned with saffron, it can be a combination of chicken, vegetables and seafood, or a combination of sausages, rabbit and meat with chickpeas. Each region will have its own variation. Spaniards usually eat paella at midday and preferably at a restaurant by the beach, but it is served to tourists at dinner time too.

Although many people consider paella the most typical of Spanish dishes, its origins are fairly recent. The first paella was prepared in Valencia in the late 19th century. The Spanish dish which many claim

Paella, a wonderful dish of rice cooked with seafood, chicken and aromatic herbs and spices, is considered by many foreigners as the Spanish 'national dish'.

to be most national or traditional is a meat stew called *cocido* in Madrid, *potaje* in Andalusia and *escudella* by the Catalans. Three basic ingredients – meats, legumes and vegetables – produce a dish usually served in three courses. The broth is served first, then the vegetables, and the meal ends with the meats which Spaniards sometimes shred and mix to form what is called *pringa*.

Seafood

Northern Spain is famous for its seafood. One of its specialities is *merluza* (hake), prepared in two ways: either *a la gallega* (steamed in a Galician paprika sauce) or *a la sidra* (in a tangy Asturian cider sauce).

Scallops, the symbol of pilgrims to Santiago, and *pulpo* (fried octopus) are popular in Galicia which is also famous for its oysters, lobsters and crabs. Trout and salmon are a treat in Asturias (a region also famous for its hearty stews).

Basque cuisine, arguably the best in Spain, combines the use of fresh fish from the Atlantic with delicious sauces, doubtless the result of proximity to France. *Changurro* (stuffed king crab) is a speciality of this area where you will also find an interesting fish dish called *bacalao al pil-pil* (cod fried in garlic and covered in a green sauce made from the fish gelatin).

Fish is a favourite ingredient in Spanish cooking. The number of fishermen on the costas *ensure a steady supply of seafood.*

The last time we stopped in a hotel in San Sebastian, we came down to the dining room at 9.30 pm to find it completely empty apart from the waitresses. When we asked to see the menu, the one serving us shrugged her shoulders and reeled off the evening's offerings, but her 'Spanish' (Euskera, the Basque language) was such that we didn't understand one word. We shrugged in turn and nodded our acceptance, and a plate of spinach cooked with garlic appeared in front of us. It didn't look too wonderful but tasted delicious. Next came a clay pot filled with fish cooked with tomatoes, onions and aubergines, and finally a small bowl full of luscious black cherries. By the time we were drinking our coffee, the restaurant was packed with Spaniards, all eating exactly what we had had with evident gusto. Spaniards do enjoy their food, so if you are in doubt about what to order, in most instances you can safely go along with the waitress's suggestions. Pleasant surprises await you if you are adventurous and try the recommendations.

Local trout grilled over hot coals is a delicious speciality in the Pyrenees, and Western Andalusia is renowned for shrimps, prawns and crayfish, and excellent fried fish crisp on the outside and succulent within.

Meats and Hams

The classic dishes in Castile are *cordero* (lamb) or *cochinillo* (suckling pig) roasted in wood or clay ovens. Casa Botin in Madrid, called the world's oldest restaurant by the *Guinness Book of Records*, specializes in both of these, cooked in ovens dating back several centuries.

The mountainous districts of Salamanca are famous for their hams and sausages. The cured hams of Trevelez and Jabugo, the *chorizo* (spicy paprika sausage) and *morcilla* (blood sausage) of Granada and Burgos are all renowned.

Game is abundant throughout the northern provinces. Meat cooked *a la llosa* (scared on a slate slab over coals) is characteristic in the Pyrenees where *civet*, an aromatic stew prepared with wild boar or goat, can also be found.

The food of Extremadura is true peasant fare conditioned by poverty. Pigs form its basis and no parts are spared, including the *criadillas* (testicles). The charcuterie products are excellent, notably the cured hams from Montanchez. Certain dishes may appal foreigners as well as Spaniards from other parts of Spain, particularly those involving *ranas* (frogs) and *lagartos* (lizards), the latter usually served with an almond sauce.

Cheeses

Usually only to be bought in the area where it is made, the range of Spanish cheeses is impressive. However, this range cannot be compared with the variety available in either France or England. Most of the cheeses are grouped together and simply called Manchego. A good Manchego viejo is almost the equal of Italian Parmesan. In addition to the Manchegos, the hard cheeses of La Mancha are delightful when well matured, and Cabrales, a sheep's cheese rather like Roquefort, is worth looking for.

Sweets

It may surprise you to discover that convents supply a variety of almond- or honey-based sweets, pastries and cakes. Saint Teresa devised *yemas* (egg-yolk sweets) which were originally distributed to the poor. However, their production became a profitable industry for the nuns, so now you can ring the bell of the convent, greet the nun (usually hidden) with '*Ave Maria Purissima*', and after this formality, proceed to order your *yemas* or *bizcochos* (sponge biscuits) or whatever else may appear on the list pinned to the entrance of the convent. They are usually delicious.

RESTAURANTS

Standards will vary, as will the prices of food and wine, from exclusive, expensive, immaculately served meals in beautiful surroundings down to small, more intimate, usually family-run affairs where the service can be extremely slow during high season. A single waiter (usually the son) races from table to table whilst Papa takes the orders and Mama (assisted by daughter) deals with the kitchen. They are doing their best, so getting impatient with delays is a waste of time.

In most instances, it is advisable to book a table for whatever time you want to eat. You may nevertheless have to wait a while, but at least you are certain of getting a table. Most restaurants are prepared to start serving meals quite early. However, if you do not want to be surrounded by other foreigners and prefer a more Spanish ambience, remember that locals seldom have lunch before 2 or even 3 pm, and dinner before 9 or 10 pm.

In the family-run bar or restaurant, don't be shocked if your food is brought to the table by the eight-year old son or daughter of the owner. As young children cannot be left at home unsupervised, they often spend their evenings with Mama and Papa in the restaurant. Rather than allowing the children to get bored with nothing to do, the parents may encourage participation in the running of the family business.

Merenderos

'Cheap and cheerful' best describes these numerous small country restaurants which usually serve meals outdoors in the summer. Some may have a set menu giving you a choice of starter, main course and dessert, with half a bottle of wine or mineral water for as little as 600 pesetas per person (about £4 or US$7). The house wines are drinkable, but you may prefer to pay a bit more and order one you like better.

Tapas Bars

Perhaps most typical of Spain, these bars are favourite meeting places

Tapas *bars tucked away in back streets may look ordinary but are worth checking out. You can have an enjoyable meal in a* tapas *bar, sampling various Spanish dishes in small portions.*

125

for young and old alike. Some display the day's offerings in dishes ranged along the top of the counter, others will merely have a blackboard up on a wall listing the goodies on offer. You either sit at the bar and make your selection there, or find yourself a table and what you order will be brought to you.

The selection can be a gastronomic delight: thinly sliced aubergines or courgettes deep fried in light batter; thinly sliced mushrooms or artichokes grilled with lemon, oil and garlic; grilled sardines, or crisply fried *pescaditos* or *boccarones*, small fish of different types; *almeja* (mussels and tiny clams) or *calamares* (squid) either *a la plancha* (grilled whole) or *a la romana* (cut into rings and deep fried in batter); crispy salads; delicious meatballs or a simple *tortilla* (an omelette made with onions, potatoes and garlic). It's a good idea to ask the waiter if there are any 'specials' available ... one evening we feasted on sardines, deboned, opened flat and fried in light batter.

Most visitors find *tapas* bars a treat as they are given an opportunity to try any number of different typical dishes. Including wine, the bill seldom comes up to more than 1000 pesetas a head (approximately £6 or US$10).

Tipping
If you are satisfied with the service in a restaurant, a 10% tip is adequate, less if you eat *tapas* at a bar when it is usual to round off the bill to the nearest hundred pesetas. (Incidentally, whilst on the subject of tipping, taxi drivers and hotel porters will expect small tips for carrying your luggage; barbers 100 pesetas for a haircut, and ladies' hairdressers twice that amount for a wash and set.)

DRINKING
Although Spaniards are comparatively heavy drinkers – they may start the day off with a *carajillo* (black coffee laced with a large tot of brandy) for breakfast, polish off a bottle of wine with their *bocadillo* (sandwich) at lunch time, and sit in the bars drinking all evening – you

126

will seldom see a drunken Spaniard.

Prices of local wines, liqueurs and brandies are extremely cheap and this sometimes gives foreigners a headache ... literally! Particular care should be taken when ordering a whiskey, gin or rum-based drink ... the price may seem comparatively high but the measure you get will be far more generous than you may be used to!

A pleasant summer drink is *sangria*, a fruit and wine punch diluted with lemonade but sometimes given a 'kick' by the addition of one or two hard liquors. Don't order *sangria* if you are in a 'low dive' because it may be laced with very cheap, poor-quality alcohol which is quite likely to make you ill.

On the whole Spaniards are unpretentious in their drinking habits, buying their wines from huge barrels marked *tinto* (red), *blanco* (white) or *rosado* (pink). However, recent promotion of Spanish wines has made them fashionable, and bottles are now labelled in accordance with other European standards, stating the year of the

production rather than the 'age' in so many years.

Spain's largest wine-growing area, La Mancha, produces the cheaper variety of wine from Valdepans. At the other end of the scale are the excellent red wines from Rioja, some of which have a full-bodied woody flavour from being matured for up to eight years in casks made of oak.

Sherries have, of course, always been popular with Spaniards and foreigners alike. However, the English have dominated the sherry trade in Jerez de la Frontera since the 16th century. Many of the labels are foreign, Harvey and Sandeman for example. Classic dry sherry is called *fino*; *amontillado* is deeper in colour and taste; and *oloroso* is more like a sweet dessert wine. Another aperitif is *manzanilla*, a fortified wine with a faint tang of the sea. Sherries are considered an ideal accompaniment to *tapas* but many Spaniards will also drink

Liquors are generally cheaper in Spain than elsewhere in Europe. Spanish wines are of very high quality and can be purchased from grocery stores.

them with their meals.

Spanish brandies make a perfect ending to a Spanish meal but you may prefer to try an *anis* (a drink which tastes of aniseed), either *seco* (dry) or *dulce* (sweet). A popular after-dinner drink is called *sol y sombra* (sun and shade). It is a combination of brandy and *anis* and the proportions can be varied to suit your taste. Another popular liqueur is the rather sweet *ponche caballero* which comes in a silver-coated bottle.

– Chapter Nine –

EDUCATION, HEALTH, LAW AND ORDER

IT'S FOR MY OWN SAFETY

In recent years, tremendous progress has been made in connection with improving educational facilities, and health and emergency services.

EDUCATION

A 1970 Act made it compulsory for children to attend school between the ages of six and fourteen, and this basic schooling is available at no cost. After completing basic education, the pupils are faced with a choice of either three years of further academic study, plus another one-year course intended to prepare them for university, or two-year courses providing a general introduction to things like clerical work or hairdressing, which can be followed up with another two-year course offering specialized vocational training.

From being one of the poorest nations in respect of schools and universities, Spanish standards can now be favourably compared with the rest of Europe.

Kindergartens

Most parents send their children to nursery schools either to ensure that they get a good start, or simply to get the children out of the way during the day. It is a common sight in some of the larger cities to see a crocodile of small children tethered together with a rope being led along by an adult. These are not miniature criminals being led off to jail; merely nursery schoolchildren being taken for a walk by their teacher – tethered together for their own protection!

Nursery children going for a walk. The rope keeps them from straying.

131

Schools

Apart from state run schools, which accept foreign students, there are also a number of foreign schools available. Completely English or American ones are run on exactly the same systems as schools in England and America, with the same targets, and the standards are usually very good.

Some parents prefer to send their children to English/Spanish bilingual schools where Spanish language classes are usually very demanding whereas the English classes are geared towards second language learners. It isn't easy to find schools which prepare children equally well in both languages. Also Spanish standards for mathematics and science are considerably higher than in the United States, which could make things difficult for a new student.

Some schools offer school lunches to students, but not all of them do. If you live near the school, your children can come home for lunch. Otherwise they can bring packed lunches. There is no hard and fast rule.

'Bedtime!'

This word creates problems for foreign parents who feel their children of school-going age should retire to bed at a reasonable time in order to be fresh and alert for lessons the following day. 'It's hard to get kids to bed at a decent hour,' says a Canadian, 'when all the neighbourhood children are still out with their bikes and skateboards. School-going children are often out with their friends till 9 or 10 during term-time, and till 11 or 12 during summer!'

Universities

The number of university students more than tripled in the sixties, and by the early seventies nearly a quarter of a million students attended one of the 30-odd universities in Spain, a few of which are run by the Church and one by Opus Dei. The two biggest, the Complutense in Madrid and the Central in Barcelona, are responsible for more than half the total number of students. Spanish universities make a clear distinction between academic and practical studies. Conventional faculties and colleges offer traditional disciplines which may take five or six years. University schools offer courses for training as teachers, nurses and the like. The universities have more than half a million undergraduates and graduate unemployment has been a problem since the mid-seventies.

HEALTH SERVICES
Nowadays most foreigners have nothing but praise for the services available and even in emergencies, ambulances arrive promptly and patients are whisked to the appropriate hospital or clinic for treatment.

Hospitals
Spanish hospitals usually provide an extra bed in the patient's room. This is for the family member who accompanies the patient to hospital. Qualified nurses handle the skilled work and the patient's family is expected to attend to the patient's comfort. Nowadays some of the more modern hospitals or clinics in the larger cities no longer expect a patient's family to provide this service, but many still have the extra bed in case it is desired. Most hospitals nowadays are well staffed and the standard of specialized treatment is high.

Minor ailments can be treated by private doctors, either at their clinic or, if necessary, at home. Spanish doctors are still quite prepared to pay daily calls on patients in their homes if they feel the patient requires such attention.

Qualified pharmacists often offer medical advice and, if you know which medicine is effective for your particular ailment, you will be able to purchase it over the counter from a pharmacy without incurring the expense of a doctor's visit beforehand.

For national health services, you have to register with a specific doctor.

Social Welfare

Reciprocal arrangements exist between most of the European countries, and if a foreigner is entitled to free medical and dental care in his own country, he will usually find he can get it just as easily in Spain. Friends (retired on the Costa Blanca) who are entitled to these facilities say that the service is excellent, the doctors usually understand foreign languages, and the equipment in the hospitals and dental clinics is very up-to-date. However, friends working in Madrid complain that emergency services are depressing and often overcrowded, and that there could be months of waiting for X-rays, operations, etc. in the social security system. They consider it mandatory to have a separate insurance to cover most medical care.

Public Health

'Don't drink water from the tap or eat uncooked vegetables' used to be good advice when travelling about in Spain and people who did not heed it often succumbed to violent attacks of 'Spanish tummy' which was not just the result of a change of climate and diet, but due to slack attention to hygiene. After the tragedy of what was called the 'toxic syndrome' in the early eighties which claimed over 300 lives, food inspection and regulations controlling standards of hygiene in bars and restaurants were tightened up and one no longer needs to avoid salads when dining out.

Now that Spain is a member of the European Community, all food and drink has to be labelled in accordance with EC standards, clearly showing expiry dates, etc.

Pharmacies

Each pharmacy in Spain is owned and operated by a qualified pharmacist who is not permitted to own more than one shop. All the pharmacies in a certain area take it in turn to remain open as a *farmacia de guardia* for 24 hours a day, and a small notice on the door of a closed pharmacy will tell you which one is open on that particular day

Buying medicine in a farmacia *is easy as the pharmacist is usually helpful and friendly. You usually do not need a prescription to get many types of medicines.*

or night. Pharmacies stock medicines, medical products, hair sprays, cosmetics and soaps. Also baby foods which are sold in supermarkets and hypermarkets as well. Medicines purchased outside Spain can probably be replaced by a Spanish equivalent, but you should be able to give the pharmacist the brand and manufacturer's name, and most important the formula. If the pharmacist does not have the required medicine in stock, he can usually get it quite quickly by phoning wholesalers in the vicinity.

Most foreigners are amazed at how easy it is to get medicines (which would require a doctor's prescription elsewhere) without any prescription from a pharmacy in Spain, and usually at a fraction of the cost.

Voluntary Help Groups

Independent help groups operate in several Costa Blanca municipalities and similar groups will be found in other parts of Spain. Volunteers will provide neighbourly assistance in cases of emergency and during rehabilitation periods after hospitalization, visit the elderly who may be house-bound and, if necessary, do the grocery shopping. In fact, as the name implies, HELP is there to be of help to you whenever needed. It also has a supply of medical and orthopaedic equipment which can be borrowed.

Spanish 'Cure-alls'

Spaniards believe you will get sick if you don't wear your slippers, or if you stay in a draught, or get your 'kidneys' cold. When you are sick, their 'cure-all' is either hot milk laced with brandy and honey or warm lemon juice with honey. These can be whole-heartedly recommended … they taste wonderful regardless of how effective they may be!

Red Cross Posts

You will find these posts at intervals along the main highways, and usually in the larger villages as well. They are staffed and equipped

to deal with accidents on the spot.

Instead of doing their military service (250,000 young men are conscripted into the army every year for a minimum service of 12 months) young men can opt for a longer period of service with the Red Cross. After six weeks' training, the 'volunteer' is presented with a pair of socks and a pair of underpants! The rest of his clothing, plus cost of food and accommodation, is the responsibility of fund-raisers in the town where he serves. However, due to recent changes in the conditions for military service, the Red Cross is experiencing a shortage of staff, especially ambulance drivers.

Much of the Red Cross funds is raised by 'flag' sales to motorists waiting at traffic lights or in summer traffic jams, but this can be hazardous. Some towns prefer to provide the necessary money from public funds after boys were involved in accidents whilst attempting to sell flags at crossroads.

MILITARY SERVICE

The death rate amongst Spanish youngsters doing their 'mill' is 10 times higher than for any other European national serviceman. Selection is made by a random process. The fate of the young men is decided by a nationally televised lottery when 365 balls inscribed with day and month are selected one by one. It sometimes seems unfair that one youngster has to serve his country whilst a neighbour born on another day has the chance to continue his studies towards a lucrative career. Quite a few young soldiers attempt to commit suicide but less than a quarter are successful.

FIRE BRIGADE

Fire fighters are kept busy in the summer in areas with pine forests. In most places, there are restrictions about when and where you can burn your garden rubbish and some areas insist that you advise the municipality and acquire their permission before lighting up. In any case, fires are strictly forbidden during the summer months when the countryside is particularly vulnerable to sparks starting off dangerous forest fires.

LAW AND ORDER

Although the amount of crime committed in Spain is lower than in most of Europe, the police force in Spain is very large, the ratio being about one police officer for every 250 inhabitants. Urban areas are patrolled by three different sorts of force.

Policia Municipal

These are recruited locally and paid for by the town or city council concerned. They are responsible for traffic and parking and upholding local bylaws, and are found in any town with a population of over 5000.

Policia Nacional

Uniformed forces employed by the government, organized on quasi-military lines, are found in towns of more than 20,000 inhabitants or highly industrialized centres. These have replaced the hated Policia Armada of Franco's era, and because of the change in their outlook and attitude, they are now quite popular with the public.

Cuerpo Superior de Policia

As the name implies, this is the most senior of the urban forces and consists of plain clothes officers who devise and administer the policing policies in each area.

Guardia Civil

The history of the Guardia Civil can be traced back to 1844 when the

Staying within the law in Spain is easy as policemen are friendly and helpful.

government set it up to combat banditry. Today its main duties are to patrol the countryside, the highways and frontiers, and act as customs officers. A few foreigners appear to fear the Guardias, but if you are a law-abiding citizen, you will find them extraordinarily civil and very helpful in times of need.

STAYING WITHIN THE LAW

For some inexplicable reason, many foreigners coming to reside in Spain appear to believe that Spanish rules and regulations are not intended for them. They will build houses and pools without acquiring the necessary permits, they will ignore traffic regulations such as roundabouts and one-way streets and parking restrictions, and then act the injured party when they are suddenly hauled up and either taken to court or made to pay a fine. Pleading ignorance is no excuse because there is no reason to be ignorant of the law ... anyone you talk to will be more than willing to give you advice. The important thing is to get the right advice and follow it.

Keeping within the law will ensure a cooperative attitude from the Spanish authorities. If you do the right thing, so will they. They are not out to hound you unless you take it upon yourself to ignore their laws.

The authorities even have been known to turn a blind eye on law infringement for a period of time if they believe they have a good reason to do so. For example, a yacht owner, having got into debt, decided to make some money by chartering his boat. This is strictly not allowed, but no one seemed to mind nor was any attempt made to stop him. Then one day, the police pounced on him. When he asked why, he was told, 'You have made enough money to pay all your debts so now you must stop breaking the law.'

Chapter Ten

RESORTS, LEISURE AND TRAVEL

From being an arid landscape with little settlement, the shoreline of Spain was transformed into bustling towns and glamorous resorts. As has already been stressed on several occasions in this book, the coastal areas most popular with foreigners are least typical of Spain. The Mediterranean coastline was transformed beyond all recognition in the years following the Second World War. Between the years 1959 and 1973 the number of visitors increased tenfold and land prices soared. Land which Spaniards had regarded as practically worthless, being either rocky or sandy, suddenly became very valuable.

THE TOURIST BOOM

Tourism provided material advantages for property developers, shop-keepers and villagers along the coast. Jobs became available for those without any skill, and the skilled artisan found his products snapped up in no time. But the tourist boom was not an unmitigated blessing. It was too sudden and too rapid. Spaniards were confronted with a new way of life where men walked around with wallets bulging with money and women walked about half-naked. They had to learn to deal with new concepts like credit cards and dishwashers, and for some of them it proved too much. The result in many cases was shock. Men in particular suffered from insomnia, listlessness and breathlessness and hospital wards had to be enlarged to cater for these patients, most of whom were teenage males who had gone to work on the coast.

Community Spirit

As the face of Spain changed, so did the Spaniards. Intemperate, egotistical individuals, intolerant of any views other than their own are less in evidence these days. Although Spaniards may still talk loudly and emphatically, ignore traffic lights and behave arrogantly, they have developed more of a 'community spirit'. However, Spaniards of coastal areas are very different from those in rural areas, or in the cities. Drive a few miles inland from one of the coastal resorts and you will find small villages where the local bar will have its share of old men wearing black berets, sitting with a glass of wine playing dominoes. You feel as though you have stepped back about 50 years into history, and characters like those described by Hemingway in his Spanish books are still in evidence.

MODERN RESORTS

With increased prosperity, more Spaniards are beginning to take an interest in their own resorts. Every year there is an increase in the number of Madrid and other Spanish registered cars in resort areas which up until recently were avoided by holidaying Spaniards, and in the number of Spaniards who have bought holiday homes in some of the resorts.

Beaches

If you are expecting to find long stretches of white sand, palm trees, warm waters and few people, you will find the Spanish beaches a disappointment. They are extremely popular with Northern Europeans, particularly Germans who have no sea comparable to the Mediterranean. Beaches which are made of fine sand can be so crowded during the summer that finding a few square inches to call your own is often quite difficult. However, if you travel further from the towns, you may come across quiet spots.

In many places, the Tourist Board has taken care to provide shower facilities at frequent intervals and a system of rating for cleanliness so that visitors can avoid swimming in waters considered polluted. There are areas specifically designated for those who like to go topless or swim in the nude. These are clearly indicated by sign posts.

Water Sports

Sailing and boating are very popular along the Mediterranean coast and there are hundreds of marinas and clubs available. Spain's best-known sailing enthusiast is King Juan Carlos who keeps his fleet of boats in Majorca.

Most resort beaches will have areas designated for wind surfing or water- and jet-skiing. This makes the swimming safer for those who are not interested in such sports. Scuba-diving and underwater fishing are very popular, but make sure your presence in the water is clearly indicated with a marker buoy.

LEISURE

The older-generation Spaniard may still prefer to sit at home or in a bar and watch a soccer match on TV or devote leisure time to strolling gently before settling down to a gastronomic feast. However, the young people of Spain these days are as health-conscious as most other youngsters. Far more time and money are spent on sport in one form or another than most other forms of amusement. As a result, Spain has produced its share of world-class golfers, tennis players and, needless to say, football teams.

Football

Surprisingly enough, football in Spain has more *aficionados* than even bullfighting. It is in fact considered to be THE national sport, and football has a greater following in Spain than it does even in England, where the game originated.

The most popular teams are Real Madrid whose home is the 130,000 spectator Santiago Bernabeu Stadium and Atletico Madrid whose Vicente Calderon Stadium is located on the outskirts of town. The best team in the Basque area is the Club Atletico Bilbao and fixtures for games are listed in the local press. Catalans, however, are perhaps the most active of all Spanish *futbol* supporters. When the Barcelona team, 'Barça', wins, everyone goes wild with joy. A recent victory for the team was celebrated for an hour or more with horns being tooted, rockets going off and fans waving flags and cheering.

Football matches are played on Saturday and Sunday evenings (to avoid the mid-afternoon heat) and tickets are not considered expensive at 3000 pesetas (approximately £15 or US$30) for an average seat. The last match of the season, which lasts from September through till June is the Copa Real or 'King's Cup'. All the bars with television will have a *futbol* match on their screens during the weekend, and supporters, unable to acquire tickets for the game, will crowd into the bars and scream their pleasure whenever a goal is scored by their team. People gamble on football results through a tote called Quiniela.

Futbol sala is the latest craze in nearly all the bigger towns and cities. Run as a commercial business, it is a form of football played indoors, usually in large underground car parks converted for the purpose. A very fast game and highly competitive, teams of youths form for the season and league games are organized.

Even very small villages will have at least one football field which children can use if the local school does not have one. In one small seaside resort on the Costa Blanca a sum of 10 million pesetas was approved by the town council for the creation of a football school whereas only one-tenth of that amount was approved to fund a home help service via the Red Cross for the elderly, handicapped or disabled. Teaching children to play football therefore would appear to be high on the list of priorities!

Winter Sports

Excellent skiing and winter sports facilities are scattered throughout Spain's mountainous regions, from the Picos of Europa in the west across to the Pyrenees which offer popular resorts such as Baqueira-Beret near Lerida and Candanchi in Aragon. You can also ski close to Madrid at Navacerrada, Valcoto and Valdesqui, and at Solynieve in the Sierra Nevada, probably the most popular area. Costs for skiing in Spain are much lower than at any of the Continental resorts, and accommodation and food are also much more reasonably priced.

Mountaineering and climbing are also popular and there are plenty of challenges throughout Spain in terms of difficulty of ascent. However, don't expect the rescue back-up service that you would get in the rest of Europe. In Spain climbing is an individual affair and carried out at your own risk. Better join a club and check out local conditions before setting off – remember brown bears and wolves still exist and they may not enjoy being disturbed. So take care!

Hunting

Spain is famous as a 'paradise' for hunters due to its climatic range, the variety of its wildlife and the many traditional methods of hunting both large and small game. Numerous national parks and game preserves exist where natural resources are protected. Big game includes deer, stag, ibex, roebuck, mountain goat, boar, wolf, moun-

tain sheep, bear and lynx. Lynx is completely protected having become scarce, and hunting bear is restricted.

There are literally thousands of private reserves for small game where most of the hunting takes place. Among the small game you will find partridge, water fowl, dove, quail, bustard, grouse, rabbit, hare and pheasant.

Many traditional methods of hunting exist in Spain, some on horseback, some on foot, others involving groups of hunters with horses, assistants, hounds and handlers. However the only method permitted in the national reserves and game preserves is called *resecho* where a single hunter, sometimes accompanied by a guide, searches for game on foot, a true test of his knowledge and physical ability.

Small game is sought by a lone hunter who will shoot at anything his dog starts. The most popular method used in hunting the Spanish red partridge is 'beating up'. Preparing such an occasion requires great knowledge of the partridge and the terrain which is divided into plots, in each of which a dozen or so blinds are set up. In these partridge drives, nothing is left to chance. Everything is calculated and arranged so that helpers, loaders, beaters and hunters all come together at the right time and in the right place. This type of Spanish hunt is internationally famous and, unless you have taken part in one of these traditional drives, you really shouldn't boast about being a 'hunter' in Spain!

'Shooting'

Many foreigners are shocked by the sight of hundreds of small dead birds piled on the side of country roads and wonder if such slaughter is really necessary. The excuse for this seemingly indiscriminate massacre is that farmers are protecting crops on their fruit trees. However, the sight of so many little corpses lying by the roadside leaves one with the impression that local 'huntsmen' are amusing themselves by blasting away at anything that flies. If you are fond of hiking in the hills, you should make sure you don't wander into areas where such 'huntsmen' abound.

Black and white signs hanging from trees by the roadside or in forests saying '*Coto privado de caza*' mean 'private hunting area'. So it is advisable to keep clear.

Fishing

With its 3200 kilometres (2000 miles) of coastline and more than 20 times as many miles of rivers and streams, plus all the dams and reservoirs scattered around the country, Spain offers unlimited possibilities for the keen fisherman. Spanish salmon rivers are found throughout the Cantabrian range and along the coast of Galicia, and trout can be caught in the upper reaches of practically any river in Spain. Salt-water fishing can be done from the shore, or from boats, or underwater. All forms of fishing require licences and can only be pursued during open seasons, with limitations on minimum sizes.

You can fish from almost any part of the Spanish shoreline.

TRAVEL

You can get around Spain in a number of ways, including trains, buses and even bicycles, should you so desire.

Trains

In general, RENFE, the government-run railroad, is below par by European standards. The first high-speed train between Madrid and Seville made its debut just in time for the 1992 Expo. Long-distance runs are mostly made at night and can be very slow. Train travel, however, is probably the most economical method of getting around Spain. First- and second-class seats are reasonably priced but food and drink in the dining cars and bars are over-priced and usually uninspiring.

If you are an *aficionado* of antique trains, RENFE operates the luxurious turn-of-the-century Al-Andalus Express which makes two-day and three-day trips for sightseeing purposes in Cordoba, Granada and Seville, and also runs from Pamplona to Santiago de Compostela along the Way of St James during summer.

Kings and queens used to travel on these trains which have been beautifully restored down to the smallest detail. Even the sleeping compartments complete the mood of old time elegance.

Way of Saint James

Saint James is said to be buried at Santiago de Compostela, which in the Middle Ages was considered the third most important Christian shrine. In the 12th century as many as two million pilgrims travelled the road to Compostela from all over Europe. In 1990 it was estimated that as many as 14,000 pilgrims travelled the same route on foot, with many more covering the same road by coach and car.

Buses

Private companies run the bus services which can range from knee-crunching basic to luxurious. Fares tend to be lower than for rail travel and you can be fairly sure of finding buses to take you to destinations not serviced by trains.

Eurolines/National Express consortium has regular coach services from London to more than 45 destinations in Spain. These journeys take about 26 hours to Barcelona or 32 hours to Madrid and run twice a week throughout the year. Fares are reasonable and the coaches provide TV entertainment and toilet facilities. There are also coach services linking the various cities.

Bicycles

Bicycle trips require careful planning because of the mountainous country and crowded roads you are likely to encounter. 'The Route of El Cid' prepared by the Tourist Office is a 20-day cycling tour which can be a great help should you wish to pedal from Burgos to Valencia.

Cyclists have to be careful on the road, but cycling is a very popular sport in Spain as well as being a form of travel. Other road users are unusually wary of cyclists, automatically slowing down when overtaking, etc.

Cars

In the summer season, cars travel at snail's pace, nose to tail along the coast. *Autopistas* operated on a toll system tend to be less congested. Most places have traffic police to deal with congestions and to make sure that parking restrictions are adhered to. Until recently Spaniards were in the habit of leaving their cars wherever convenient, often double or even triple parked. In Madrid, when the Spanish equivalent of English clamps was first introduced, it almost caused a major riot. People demonstrated and many who attacked the clamps with sledge-hammers were taken to court.

Perhaps careless parking by tourists merely reflects their desire to follow the Spanish example but increased surveillance by local traffic police and designation of properly marked and controlled parking areas have improved the circulation of traffic generally.

Pedestrian Crossings

Rather than ensuring a safe crossing for pedestrians, these can be extremely hazardous and you are advised to be particularly careful when crossing roads. Recently three elderly Spanish women were mown down by a car in Benidorm whilst attempting to cross a dual carriage way at a point described as a 'pedestrian crossing'. The vehicle in this case was a Madrid-registered car driven by a Spaniard. Many drivers ignore the presence of pedestrians even if they are actually on the crossing, and accidents are frequent because some drivers also ignore speed restrictions. Some towns and villages provide traffic police at pedestrian crossings to ensure that pedestrians can cross safely and in some cities you will find the equivalent of 'WALK/DON'T WALK' lights on street corners. However, wherever you are, you really must approach even designated crossings with extreme caution.

Blowing Whistles

Policemen in other countries usually refrain from blowing their whistles except in moments of urgency when trying to prevent a crime. In Spain, all traffic police are equipped with whistles which they blow continuously, making it very difficult at times to work out what they are trying to achieve. Are you meant to stop? Are you meant to go on? You must watch the policeman carefully to find out his intention, which is more easily identified by his hand or arm movements.

Most traffic policemen are very helpful. We were once thoroughly lost in Madrid during rush hour and stopped by the side of a policeman controlling traffic at a busy intersection. We knew the address we were looking for was close but explained that we had been unsuccessful in our search, could he tell us how to get there? He climbed off his pedestal and scrambled into the back seat of our car and proceeded to direct us to our destination ... leaving the busy intersection to its fate! We offered him a few pesetas when he got out to pay for a taxi to take him back to his post, but he refused with a smile, stopped the first car that passed, climbed in and cheerfully told the driver to deposit him back at his busy intersection!

Flashing Headlights

You may also find yourself confused by flashing headlights. In England, if a car flashes its headlights at you, you can safely assume that the driver is indicating 'Go ahead'. Don't imagine this is true in Spain where flashing headlights can mean just about anything, most frequently 'Get out of my way!' Sometimes a car coming towards you from the opposite direction will flash its headlights; this is meant to warn you that there is a traffic patrol ahead, or that there has been an accident. So, whatever it may mean, you should slow down when another car flashes its headlights at you.

Driving in Spain

When in Spain, you might find it necessary to drive the way Spaniards do. They tend to be aggressive drivers, cutting in and out of lines, paying little attention to traffic rules or the needs of other road-users. When you approach that amber light and your instinct tells you to apply your brakes, first look in your rear-view mirror to make sure you do not have a Spaniard close behind you. You might find yourself being rear-ended unless you step on the accelerator and zoom right on through! In fact it is as well to drive with greater care than usual, keeping an eye on your rear-view mirror, in order to avoid unnecessary repairs. If you happen to get involved in an accident with a Spaniard, chances are that you will be found 'guilty' and fined, no matter who actually caused the accident.

Autopistas

Motorways in Spain are extensive, well-surfaced but expensive, unlike those of England and Germany which are free. The rates have been going up pretty regularly each year, and 100 kilometres (62

Autopistas *are generally well maintained and the fastest way to move from one town to another. However, they are expensive.*

miles), more or less, will cost you 1000 pesetas now (£6 or US$10). The speed limit on the *autopistas* in Spain is 120 kph or 75 mph.

Rest Areas

Like in other countries, you are not allowed to stop on the *autopistas*. There are areas every now and then where you can get petrol and buy a wide range of refreshments. Some areas have proper restaurants and serve regular meals; almost all will display a selection of *tapas* at the counter. Apart from a full range of soft drinks, you may be surprised to find you can buy beer and wine just as easily, even though drink-driving offences are not treated lightly! However, it is wise not to leave your car unattended. Windows are frequently smashed and anything left lying on the seats removed. Also beware of people asking advice about which route to follow. They may produce a map and make you peer at it closely. Whilst you are thus distracted, an accomplice will snatch whatever is handy and run.

Modern-day Highwaymen

Tourists are particularly vulnerable victims to modern-day highwaymen. Unaware that their travel plans can be telephoned ahead to modern-day highwaymen who pay handsomely for descriptions of choice victims and their belongings, they naively accept advice from a friendly stranger who may recommend a particularly picturesque and traffic-free route where the bandits can prepare their ambush.

Another favourite technique is to drive alongside a foreign car and yell that a tyre is flat. When the unsuspecting holiday maker pulls over, the gang pounces. More than 1000 vehicles fall victim to such bandits every year.

National Roads

The network of national roads is well maintained but the heavy lorry traffic can slow you down tremendously. Speed limits on these roads are 100 kph (62 mph) on roads with hard shoulders on both sides, or 90 kph (56 mph) on roads in open country.

Petrol

Petrol stations are now plentiful throughout Spain and, as prices are government-controlled, they are the same anywhere you go. Most of the stations offer Regular, Super, Unleaded petrol and Diesel. Credit cards are frequently accepted, particularly along main routes.

Road Patrols

Guardias on motorcycles (often nicknamed 'heavenly twins' because they hunt in pairs) patrol the roads constantly. One is usually a trained mechanic and the other a first aider so there are times when their arrival is welcome. On the other hand, if they catch you breaking a speed limit or crossing a double white line, they are permitted to stop and fine you on the spot, allowing you a 20% discount if you pay your fine in cash! Offering them bribes is a waste of time.

You are supposed to carry your car papers, driving licence and identification at all times.

Inspeccion Tecnica de Vehiculos

If your car has Spanish plates and is over five years old, it must display a tag showing that it has passed its ITV which is the Spanish equivalent of an English MOT (Ministry of Transport test). This ITV has to be done every second year until your car is 10 years old. After that it is done every year. You risk a fine of up to 250,000 pesetas (£45 or US$250) if you are caught driving a car which doesn't display a valid ITV tag.

Chapter Eleven

BUSINESS AND WORKING CONDITIONS

WORK PERMITS

As already mentioned in Chapter Six (*Bureaucracy and Red Tape*), if you are coming from a country outside the European Community and want to work in Spain, a work permit obtainable from the ministry of labour should be high on your list of priorities. This is applicable to all types of employment: either as an employee of a Spanish company or foreign company or as a self-employed owner of a restaurant/bar or other business. You should never start any enterprise without the necessary permission or licence, or you could find yourself in a very tight corner.

SELF-EMPLOYMENT

If you work on a self-employed basis, under present EC rules you supposedly don't need a work permit, but Spanish rules do not as yet comply with the EC. You are at present still required to join the Spanish social security service, obtain a *licencia fiscal* (trade licence) and register for income tax and IVA. If you are a professional, you will usually have to become a member of the appropriate professional college. You may be given some exemptions but a written examination is usually still required.

Now that Spain has become a full member of the European Community, any foreigner from a member country can come and work freely in Spain without first acquiring a work permit.

WORKING IN AN OFFICE

Foreigners working in Spain can be divided into two basic categories: those who work in a Spanish office with Spaniards, or those who work in an international office surrounded by foreigners of their own nationality. In the former instance, there might be quite a few 'differences' for the foreigner to cope with whilst in the latter case, working conditions in the office would be very similar to those existing in one's home country and the only 'surprises' would probably occur in outside dealings with Spaniards.

Spanish Conditions

Spain's employment laws favour the employee and a standard working week is 40 hours. The traditional siesta is slowly being replaced by a shorter lunch break.

About one-sixth of Spain's 13 million workers belong to trade unions. Wage levels have been low with the result that many Spaniards used to have more than one job. However, this is now less in evidence as salaries are fast catching up with the rest of Europe.

Employers have to pay high rates for social insurance but do not have to provide pension schemes.

157

All employees are entitled to 30 days' paid holiday a year in addition to the 15 national public holidays and usually one local public holiday.

There are 14 'months' in a Spanish employment year because employees are entitled to double salary for the months of June and December.

An employee can only be dismissed for old age if it can be proved that his age restricts him from carrying out his job satisfactorily. There is no compulsory retirement age in Spain.

Meetings and Business Lunches

Rather than prolonged discussions over the telephone, Spaniards much prefer, when possible, to arrange a meeting in a cafe or a restaurant. Such meetings are usually treated as urgent and you are expected to drop everything else and come running. Business meetings are frequent occurrences and likely to be rather noisy affairs with everyone present seeming to talk at once and no one apparently prepared to listen. You will probably find yourself being constantly interrupted and you will need to develop determination in order to put your points over.

Because of this preference for conducting business matters over a meal, business lunches tend to become lengthy affairs. Spaniards loosen up when they find themselves in informal surroundings and much prefer to do business face to face. Most business deals and important decisions can be made over a breakfast, lunch or dinner. Generally speaking, the person doing the inviting pays the bill. 'Going Dutch' is uncommon in Spain except perhaps amongst *extranjeros* (foreigners) doing business with other *extranjeros*.

Office Relationships

Unlike some nationalities who do not attach much importance to building up close relationships in offices, most Spaniards much prefer to be surrounded by familiar faces. In Spain nepotism is not frowned upon because it is common practice for Spaniards to favour family members or close friends in their business dealings. The family is a pillar of Spanish society and loyalty to one's family is undoubted. So many Spaniards feel more secure employing close relatives and friends rather than comparative strangers.

The atmosphere in most offices is likely to be quite easy-going and friendly. Handshakes and back-slapping amongst men is common and the accepted norm.

Women in the Office

Career women were rare in days gone by and for a time were not taken seriously. Nowadays they are accepted quite naturally in many fields which were closed to them previously, and they are usually treated with consideration and respect. However, if you happen to want a job in a field normally restricted to men, such as selling office equipment combined with improving office efficiency, you might be greeted by

raised eyebrows and an obvious lack of enthusiasm. This attitude will change rapidly if you impress the client with your speed, efficiency and confidence.

Remember the Spanish passion for kissing. You may find yourself receiving kisses on both cheeks from a businessman whom you have never met before. Don't be offended. Even if you weren't kissed on arrival, you can be sure you will be when you leave, and although you, as a foreigner, may well prefer the more usual business-like hand-shake, you will soon learn to accept the Spanish kisses for what they are intended ... friendly greetings and farewells, nothing more!

Also, you may take time to adjust to the Spanish *tortura de la galanteria* and become embarrassed when loud comments are passed about your appearance as you walk by. This is never intended to be taken as anything but complimentary. It is not intended to be 'sexual harassment' and you would be well advised to follow the example of Spanish women who have developed the knack of acknowledging the 'compliment' in an impersonal way.

Dress

Spaniards, particularly in the cities, are fashion-conscious and like to keep up with the latest trends. They will spend a good portion of their earnings on their clothes and will invariably appear well turned out during office hours. This is usually true for both men and women. The men nowadays may not necessarily stick to conservative dark-blue or grey suits, but even if they prefer a less 'formal' appearance, you can be sure the jacket will be extremely well cut and smart. As for women, smart suits are probably still the most popular. Only in the tourist or coastal areas will you find total informality in office-wear. However, do make some enquiries about local customs before attempting to appear in your office in clothes which may be completely unsuitable.

Business Dealings with Spaniards

Most foreigners say that they find doing business with Spaniards 'straightforward' generally speaking. The 'problems' (if any) seem to arise from the Spaniard's wish to *enjoy* what he happens to be doing at any particular moment with the frequent result that he will completely forget an appointment made a few days ago in order to pursue the business being discussed with the client sitting in front of him. One of the chief complaints voiced by many foreigners is 'unpunctuality' and, as this aspect of Spanish existence is much in evidence in all spheres, you will need to learn how to deal with:

a) sudden changes of plan

b) being stood up completely with no excuses offered

c) business meetings dragging on with the result that you too will be late for your next appointment.

WORKING HOURS

The rhythm of work in Spain is very different from what Northern Europeans may be used to. Normal office hours are from 9 am to 1 or 2 pm and 5 to 7.30 or 8 pm, except for banks and post offices which do not operate in the afternoon.

One young Englishman we know, setting up an office in Barcelona, employed a young Spanish girl as secretary. He was surprised to find that although she arrived promptly each morning at eight o'clock, she would go out half an hour later without asking permission, and resume working on her return without offering any excuse for her absence. After a couple of days, he asked her for an explanation. 'I go to have my breakfast, of course!' was the surprised reply. This 'breakfast-break' is common practice not only with office-workers but also among labourers and technicians, etc.

'Coffee-breaks' (strictly timed and restricted in most other countries) are non-existent as such in Spain. Should you run out of your office to meet a business associate over a cup of coffee two or three times a day, the time spent thus will be included in 'normal office hours' and no one will think your behaviour in the least unusual.

Builders, carpenters and the like may work from 7.30 or 8 am, go for breakfast at 9 and then take two hours off between 1 and 3 pm. However, they will then continue to work until light fails.

You will be expected to adopt these hours if you work in Spain. As far as 'international business' is concerned, for instance with North America, these hours could prove to be an advantage if you take into consideration the time differences when making long-distance phone calls.

Holiday Months

August is the main holiday month when some offices may close entirely whilst others continue operating on skeleton staffs. This could prove frustrating for international companies which wish to continue operating 'as usual'. However, August is 'holiday time' all over Spain and you would therefore do well to arrange your business commitments around the fact that nothing much can be achieved during this holiday period.

You won't be able to cash money at a bank on Saturday mornings so make sure you have sufficient funds for weekends unless you are prepared to pay the higher rates at other points of exchange.

At Christmas the tempo of work begins to slow down from around 6 to 8 December and most places of work will close at midday on Christmas Eve. Boxing Day is not an official holiday but many professional offices will remain closed and not much can be achieved work-wise in fact until after Los Reyes (Twelfth Night). Some businesses may close down entirely for three weeks around Christmas and New Year.

At Easter, offices may close at midday on the Thursday preceding Good Friday and stay closed for the weekend, or even longer.

Time Off for Fiestas

In addition, other breaks in routine are becoming common. *Puentes* (bridges) develop if a fiesta happens to fall midweek. This means workers are given time off between the actual fiesta and the nearest Sunday, so if a fiesta falls on a Tuesday, offices could be shut from the Friday of the preceding week till the following Wednesday.

Foreigners sometimes find it frustrating that the holiday periods of Easter, summer and Christmas are times when least work is done in Spain. It is a good idea to get hold of a local diary and take note of all the fiesta dates in your area, thus ensuring that you won't run out of cash nor attempt the impossible when transacting business.

Main Fiestas

Christmas Day	*el dia Navidad*
New Year's Day	*el dia del Ano Nuevo*
Saint Joseph's Day	*el dia de San Jose* (19 March)
Victory Day	*el dia de Victoria* (1 March)
Holy Week	*Semana Santa*
Good Friday	*Viernes Santo*
Easter	*Pascua*

Ascension Day	*la Ascension*
Whitsun	*el Pentecostes*
Corpus Christi	*el Corpus*
Saint James	*el dia de Santiago* (25 July)
Assumption	*la Asuncion* (15 August)
Virgin of Pilar Day	*el dia de Virgen del Pilar* (12 October)
America Day	*el dia de Hispanidad* (12 October)
All Saints Day	*el dia de todos los Santos* (1 November)
Immaculate Conception & Mothers' Day	*la Concepcion* (8 December)

Chapter Twelve

LEARNING FROM EXPERIENCE

QUESTIONNAIRE

The following questionnaire was designed to assist in the compilation of personal experiences and opinions of expatriates living in Spain. The information supplied was analysed and details of responses and comments are incorporated later in this chapter. Figures in brackets have been inserted in the relevant spaces to provide a breakdown of the total responses received.

SECTION ONE: BACKGROUND. PLEASE CIRCLE OR FILL IN

1. What nationality are you?
   (48% were British; 36% North American; 12% Continental; and 4% fitted into the category of Others.)

2. What sex are you?   MALE/FEMALE
   (52% were men and 48% women.)

3. What is your age group?   a) Under 30
                                        b) Between 30 and 50
                                        c) Over 50
   (18% were under 30; 44% between 30 & 50; and 38% over 50.)

4. How long have you lived in Spain?   a) Less than a year
                                        b) One to five years
                                        c) Over five years
   (86% have lived in Spain for over five years, some for as long as 25 years; 12% one to five years and only 2% less than one year.)

5. What town or village do you live in?

6. Which of the following best describes your area?
   a) Urban
   b) Rural
   c) Coastal

   (38% lived in urban areas and 36% in coastal areas; 26% lived in rural areas.)

7. What type of accommodation do you live in?
   a) Detached house
   b) Townhouse
   c) Bungalow
   d) Flat

   (Most people lived in detached houses or flats.)

8. Do you own your property?   YES/NO
   (70% owned their properties.)

9. Do you employ domestic help?   YES/NO
   (60% employed domestic help.)

10. Are you working?
    a) Yes
    b) No
    c) Retired

    (58% worked; the rest were retired.)

11. Why did you come to Spain?
    (Please rate in order of importance, i.e. 1, 2, 3, 4, etc.)
    a) Liked the people
    b) Liked the ambience
    c) Business opportunities
    d) Climate
    e) Health
    f) Cost of living
    g) Sports facilities

    (Reasons for coming to Spain are detailed later in this chapter.)

12. How do you rate your   a) Good
    spoken Spanish?   b) Mediocre
                                     c) Weak

(70% considered their spoken Spanish good; the remaining 30% were equally divided between mediocre and weak.)

13. Can you write a letter in Spanish?   YES/NO
    (65% said yes.)

14. Have you ever taken Spanish   YES/NO
    language lessons?
    If yes, did this help you meet   YES/NO
    more Spaniards socially?
    (68% said yes, and of these 85% said the lessons helped socially.)

15. Do you have Spanish friends   YES/NO
    you know well?
    (82% said yes.)

SECTION TWO: SETTLING IN

1. Do you find Spanish lifestyle   YES/NO
   and culture surprisingly different
   from your own?
   (74% said yes, but quite a few deleted the word 'surprisingly'.)

2. In which of the following areas do   a) Work/business
   you find the difference   b) Entertainment
   most accentuated?   c) Social behaviour
                                     d) Family life
                                     e) Mannerisms
                                     f) Religion

Please specify:
(Responses analysed later in this chapter.)

3. Do you find it difficult to make   YES/NO
   friends with Spaniards?
   If yes, please specify why:
   (20% said yes; the main reason given was 'weak language'.)

4. Do you regularly socialize   YES/NO
   with Spaniards?
   (80% said yes.)

5. Are you a member of any   YES/NO
   Spanish Club?
   If yes, please specify areas of interest:
   (Only 10% said yes, of which half specified golf, the rest sports such as yachting, football, and mountain walking. One young Englishwoman admitted having joined a bullfighting club!)

6. Are your business dealings   a) Straightforward?
   with Spaniards   b) Slightly difficult?
   If b) please state the type of difficulties:
   (Of the 40% who admitted business dealings were slightly difficult, most gave 'bureaucracy, peculiar business hours and inefficiency' as the reasons.)

7. Do you eat out regularly?   YES/NO
   If yes, where do you go?   a) Restaurant
       b) *Tapas* bar/*merendero*
       c) Club
       d) Picnic
   (Of the 86% who said yes, nearly twice as many favoured restaurants as did *tapas* bars. Only 3% mentioned clubs or picnics.)

8. Do you enjoy Spanish cooking?   YES/NO
   If yes, which dishes in particular do you like?
   (96% said yes. Paella was specified more often than any other
   dish, followed by *gazpacho* (a cold vegetable soup) and roast
   suckling pig or lamb. Of the few who said no, the main reason
   given was 'too greasy'!)

9. Did you find it difficult to   YES/NO
   settle down?
   If yes, please elaborate: ·
   (Of the 14% who said yes, the main reasons given were firstly
   'language difficulties', secondly 'noise and dirt'.)

10. Do you have children at school   YES/NO
    in Spain?
    If yes, are you satisfied with   YES/NO
    educational standards and facilities?
    (Of the 30% who said yes, 93% were satisfied with standards.)

11. Have you ever had to use any of   a) Hospitals
    the following emergency services?   b) Fire department
                                          c) Traffic police
                                          d) Guardia civil
    If yes, did you find them efficient?   YES/NO
                              helpful?   YES/NO
    (Most people have had to use hospitals at one time or another and
    quite a few the Guardia. Of these more than 90% found them both
    efficient and helpful, though a few commented on the lack of
    proper nursing facilities).

12. What do you particularly like about Spain?
    (Details given later in this chapter.)

13. Are there any local customs you   YES/NO
    find particularly unusual or
    difficult to accept?
    If yes, please specify:
    (About 60% did find some local customs difficult to accept.
    Most frequently mentioned were: bullfighting, the treatment of
    animals generally, excessive fireworks, litter everywhere, and
    mañana!)

14. Is there anything you particularly   YES/NO
    miss about your home country?
    If yes, please specify:
    (Details given later in this chapter.)

15. Do you intend to return to your   a) Eventually
    home country?   b) Never
    c) Occasionally

    (Most answered occasionally.)

FURTHER COMMENTS

About 15% of the respondents were kind enough to elaborate on their
likes and dislikes and commented on aspects of Spanish culture which
they found particularly 'different' from their own. Some of these
comments are detailed below.

ANALYSIS OF RESPONSES BY REGION

Every effort was made to distribute the above questionnaire to as
many different nationalities and age groups as possible in the three
major regions: urban, rural and coastal. The survey encompassed
expatriates living and working in Madrid, Barcelona, San Sebastian,
the Costa del Sol, the Costa Blanca and Majorca.

RESPONSES COMMON TO ALL REGIONS

When one considers how different the various regions are, it is perhaps surprising that most of the questionnaires returned included many replies common to all.

Main Reasons for Coming to Spain

1. **The people**: Practically every response included an appreciation of Spanish courtesy, friendliness and generosity.
2. **The climate**: Almost everyone mentioned climate as being one of the main attractions, it being conducive to lots of outdoor activities and encouraging active interest in a variety of sports generally.
3. **The food**: Nearly everyone listed at least three dishes they particularly liked, chief amongst which were: paella, *cocido madrileno, cordero asado de Segovia* and *pulpo a la gallega*. Lots of responses specifically mentioned *tapas* as being popular.
4. **The ambience**: Most foreigners enjoy the relaxed atmosphere prevalent throughout Spain. From the responses received, it would appear that some foreigners are quick to adjust to the Spanish *mañana* and soon begin to enjoy the 'nobody is in a hurry' way of life. Strangely enough others who also claim to enjoy the 'relaxed atmosphere' are at the same time quick to voice objections about '*mañana* not meaning tomorrow'!
5. **Business Opportunities**: Mentioned last here but in fact probably the main reason for most of the 30–50 age group coming to Spain. Many people mentioned a preference for working in a country where the sunshine and warmth of both climate and people provided them with a much happier atmosphere work-wise and a better quality of life generally.

Main 'Unacceptable Customs'

1. **Bullfighting**: 50% of the responses listed bullfighting as the *only* 'custom difficult to accept'. Some went on to include censure of

171

the Spanish attitude towards animals generally. Spaniards look after their 'working animals' with care and attention but can appear unconcerned about inflicting pain and suffering on animals which do not belong to them, particularly during certain fiestas.

2. **Dirty Streets**: The selfish and inconsiderate custom of throwing papers on the ground and dumping all sorts of rubbish along the roads is considered 'disgraceful as well as being an eyesore!' by most foreigners.

3. **Smoking**: Spaniards who ignore 'No Smoking' signs and puff away merrily in between courses during meals, quite uncaring that their smoke could be offensive to other diners, are particularly unpopular with Americans!

4. **Individualism**: When it is manifested by a lack of consideration for other people in a general way, foreigners tend to interpret this characteristic as 'selfishness'. Some mention the Spanish 'reluctance to pitch in and help' when communal effort is required.

RESPONSES COMMON TO URBAN AREAS

1. **Friendly Neighbours**: Living in close proximity with one's neighbours, i.e. in apartments or townhouses, ensures the availability of numerous Spaniards with whom one can become more or less friendly quite quickly.

2. **Cost of Living**: Most foreigners claim that the cost of eating out in the big cities is high enough to prevent them from wanting to do so frequently.

3. **Trendy Fashions**: Many foreigners commented on how well-dressed most Spaniards are, and expressed amazement at the percentage of Spanish salaries which is spent on buying the latest accessories such as hats, shoes and gloves.

RESPONSES COMMON TO RURAL AREAS

1. **Seclusion**: At the cost of being somewhat isolated, converted

fincas (farmhouses) in rural areas where one can go to 'get away from it all' still seem to hold attraction for some foreigners. Having to do without electricity and putting up with only the most primitive of toilet facilities is considered a small price to pay!

2. **Beauty**: The actual beauty of the Spanish countryside can provide a never-ending source of pleasure and enjoyment throughout the different seasons.

3. **Acceptance**: Foreigners choosing to settle in small villages off the beaten track find that once the villagers are convinced of their desire to become part of village life, it doesn't take long at all before they become integrated and make friends.

RESPONSES COMMON TO COASTAL AREAS

1. Quite a few replies listed the fact that living in Spain provided an opportunity to meet not only Spaniards but also many people of different nationalities and backgrounds, thus providing *extranjeros* with easy ways of broadening their outlooks.

2. 'Too many people and too much noise' seems to be one of the responses relevant to the coastal areas which isn't surprising considering the influx of tourists during the summer and other holiday periods.

MAIN DIFFERENCES

Fifty percent of the responses gave social behaviour as being the chief area where differences occurred, with family life and work/business following quite closely.

- North Americans miss: Opportunities for young people to do odd jobs, such as baby-sitting, in order to enable them to learn the value of money; local sports teams for children of all ages; clean streets and calm traffic; respect for other people's opinions; efficiency in bureaucratic matters; the cheaper food and clothing available in the States; equal opportunities in education at every level and for everyone; and cottage cheese!

Comment: 'Spaniards jokingly expect Spain to be PERFECT by 1992 when all the highways will be completed and all the problems will solve themselves!'

Comment: 'I find that most educated Spaniards are more interested in fine arts, painting, classical music, etc. than most Americans. In the 20 years I've been here, Spain has gone from being very formal, what-will-the-neighbours-say to being more informal (dress, manners, lifestyle) and doing what one wants regardless. I have a very comfortable upper-middle-class existence similar to what it would be in my home country. However, everything one does is a challenge (which can be a bit trying). I've spent half my life here but I'll never be a Spaniard, always *La Americana* but I don't fit into 'normal' American life either! There I'm known as *La Española*!

- British people miss: Rain, especially in August; the English sense of humour; British television; general courtesy; not being able to spend Sunday morning in bed reading *The Observer*; and fish and chips!

Comment: 'What you put into a country is what you get out. No regret about living in Catalunya where I have access to everything: sea, mountains, France only two hours away, good wines. People only find problems if they try to re-create their home country, and make no effort to speak Spanish.'

Comment: 'Spain offers an exciting variety of lifestyles with a huge choice of cultural and sporting pursuits. A certain amount of broad-mindedness is essential in both business and leisure as a rigid "North European" mentality could lead to exasperation on occasions!'

Comment: 'Spaniards have little understanding of "personal space" which plays quite an important part in the behaviour of other nationalities. They tend to encroach on "personal space" by moving in on you till their face is a few inches away from your own, and if you move away, they merely follow you. This habit of proximity can be extremely disconcerting to foreigners!'

Comment: 'Dealing with Spanish justice can be frustrating. It is slow and doesn't operate from mid-July till mid-September. On the other hand, buying property, provided you take ordinary precautions, is infinitely better organized than in England. The system of a down payment which is binding for both parties speeds up the operation and avoids "gazumping" and the "domino effect" which is prevalent in the UK.'

- Continentals miss: Efficiency and straightforwardness; good shopping; lack of professional honesty; entertainment; cultural activities such as theatres and libraries (both lending and reference).

Comment: 'Difficult to get to know the Spaniards, because they have their own families and do not need other people. They seem apprehensive towards strangers and reluctant to invite people into their own homes.'

- Japanese miss: Japanese food. They apparently find life in Spain very different from life in Japan, but like the differences and find that living in Spain improves as times passes.

Comment: 'Spain has grown on me.'

The most consistent comment: 'Although my friends and I spend a lot of time complaining about Spaniards and the Spanish way of doing things, we have to admit that we would rather live in Spain and complain than have to return to our home countries!'

Chapter Thirteen

SUMMING UP

THE 'REAL SPAIN'

What is the 'Real Spain'? A gypsy caravan towed along an *autopista* behind a gleaming BMW? Pale-skinned foreigners stretched out in neat rows on some sandy beach, broiling themselves a deep shade of lobster? 'The "Real Spain" is an elusive concept,' says Eric Ellis. An 'old' country that feels 'new', transformed in a few years from a 'backward almost Third World nation to a super-slick Eurostate'.

UNCHANGING TRADITIONS

Bullfighting remains as popular as ever despite protests from animal-rights campaigners (mostly foreign). *Tapas* continue to be enjoyed and evening meals can last well into the wee hours. Nightlife on the whole only begins after midnight, and fiestas and ferias are celebrated with unabashed vigour, culminating in the massive fireworks displays which many foreigners consider totally unacceptable. 'The money spent on fireworks could be put to much better use building more schools or feeding the poor, etc.,' writes an Italian retired on the Costa Blanca. Spanish men and women still seem to lead 'separate' lives in many ways, each pursuing their 'interests' individually. They quite often give the impression of preferring the company of their own sex.

Although Spain is a fast changing country, many people in the countryside, especially, still go about their daily life in a traditional way. This farmer prefers a leisurely form of transport to modern motorized vehicles.

CHANGING TRADITIONS

Bullfights and matadors, churches and medieval villages, donkey carts and old men wearing black berets, all these things still exist; but not exclusively. Pop culture, McDonald's and Japanese investment are in evidence too.

Siestas are being phased out and the Spanish acceptance of '*Mañana* is good enough for me' is being replaced with a desire to provide prompt and efficient service in all spheres. In fact, Spain is now one of Europe's richest countries, second to Germany in the size of its foreign reserves, and one of the world's leading industrialized powers. A model for Eastern European countries, Spain has rejoined the international mainstream and the modern world.

Roads

Road works featured high on Spain's list of priorities during 1991 in order to improve chronic traffic congestion areas. *Autovias* (divided highways) now exist between Madrid and Seville, Alicante and Saragossa. Barcelona has two new ring roads, and new roads linking Seville with Cadiz, Huelva, Jerez and Cordoba enabled thousands of people to visit Expo 92 on a day trip basis from any of these cities.

Paradors and Hotels

Quite a few *paradors* (hotels) were closed during 1991 so that renovations could be carried out. New hotels have sprung up in Barcelona and Seville, all in preparation for the Olympics and Expo 92.

Promoting Culture and Natural Beauty

In years past, the emphasis was on the sunny climate and most tourist advertisements featured girls in bikinis. The tourist department is now promoting Spain as a cultural destination, and also encouraging visitors to explore 'Green Spain' (Cantabria, Asturias and Galicia) where much of Spain's natural beauty is to be found.

Spaniards are becoming more conscious of the environment. Many towns now have such bottle banks at street corners.

Private Television

Three new networks throughout most of Spain are giving the state-owned Television Española a run for its money. Many Spanish hotels now have satellite dishes permitting guests to watch programmes in English, French and German, and keep up with CNN or BBC news.

OLYMPIC GAMES

Barcelona received a major face-lift during the months preceding the 1992 Olympic Games. This included razing entire blocks of seedy buildings, restoring the cathedral and the Gaudi architectural master-pieces, constructing two new ring roads and doubling the capacity of the airport. Whether or not the Olympics produce any long-lasting effects on the rest of Spain remains to be seen, but Barcelona has certainly benefited from all the improvements.

EXPO 92

The Universal Exhibition will run in Seville for six months from 20 April ending on Columbus Day, 12 October. A 15th-century harbour and replicas of Columbus's three ships have been re-created. One hundred and four countries and Spain's 17 autonomous regions all have pavilions highlighting recent discoveries.

MADRID CULTURAL CAPITAL OF EUROPE

In addition to Barcelona and Seville, Madrid also underwent various improvements. The European Community chose Madrid as Cultural Capital for 1992 and Madrid's monuments and old buildings were restored and several new museums opened their doors. Two new theatres were built, and a permanent circus installed near the bullring. Hundreds of concerts and theatre performances featuring artists from all over the world were scheduled as part of Madrid's 1992 festivities.

FULL MEMBERSHIP OF EUROPEAN COMMUNITY

Spain still remains a law unto itself in many ways, and even though it staunchly supports unity among the nations, toeing the EC line in every way is proving more of a challenge than originally anticipated. However, ask any foreigner why he chooses to remain in Spain and the answer invariably is 'You can't beat Spain when it comes to climate and ambience and joie de vivre and relaxed, informal ways of life! We may find cause to complain, but we wouldn't dream of leaving!'

CULTURAL QUIZ

SITUATION 1

For no apparent reason your newly installed washing machine refuses to work. As it is the height of summer and you have a houseful of family and friends, you are anxious to have the situation remedied as quickly as possible. You telephone the *tecnico* (technician) and tell him your problem. He tells you he will come *'mañana'*. *Mañana* comes and goes but there's no sign of the *tecnico*. You ring again, and are told *'mañana ... seguro'* with the same lack of result. You feel a domestic crisis building up as the laundry pile increases in size. You:

A   Telephone a third time and lose your temper.

B   Telephone again but explain as sweetly as possible that you are at your wit's end because you have a baby in the house, as well as numerous other people.

C   Hop in your car and drive furiously to the *tecnico's* office in the hope of catching him there and forcing him to come back with you for immediate action.

D   Try and fix the machine yourself.

E   Go out and buy a new machine of a different make.

Comment

None of the above is likely to do you much good. A perhaps releases some of your pent-up frustration but nothing more. B merely earns you more assurances of action *mañana*. As for C, even if you can find your way to the *tecnico's* office, the chances are that he will be out so your trip will have been a waste of time. Good luck with D! It would certainly be worth making the effort if you have a bit of technical knowledge and you think there's a possibility of finding and fixing the problem, but remember if you tinker with your machine whilst it is still under guarantee, the guarantee will be invalidated. E would solve the problem, but it is an expensive way.

This is a situation to try your patience ... the *tecnico* has not been lying to you. He sincerely hopes to be able to come *mañana* and, not wanting to disappoint you, he continues to assure you that he will Perhaps the best solution is to shrug your shoulders, sit back and wait ... or go and find the nearest launderette! You could also try some hand washing.

SITUATION 2

You decide to go out for a romantic candle-lit dinner in one of the more exclusive restaurants in your area. You are having a lovely meal, accompanied by excellent local wine, and are feeling very mellow. You are looking forward to a final *café solo* and the smooth Spanish

cognac you have learned to appreciate. Your relaxed mood is unexpectedly shattered by the sound of young voices shouting and the clatter of tiny feet running between the tables. No one else seems to mind or even notice the noise. You in turn try to ignore the disturbance expecting parental discipline to descend on the children who are now playing a vigorous game of 'Catch' around your table. When you find you can no longer converse with your date without shouting, you:

A Stand up, thump the table and shout, '*Silencio, por favor!*'
B Shout for the head waiter and complain loudly and bitterly about the noisy children showing so little consideration for other diners.
C Try to locate the children's parents and suggest that they try controlling their charming offspring.
D Shout for the bill and leave the restaurant in an obvious huff.
E Order another brandy.

Comment

In fact there is little you can do to remedy this particular situation. A probably earns you surprised looks from other diners, although it might possibly have a slightly quietening effect on the children if you shout loudly enough. However, the effect would only be temporary. B may put the head waiter on the hot seat. He may not want to offend the big party to which the children belong. C is worth a try but the parents could respond in a variety of ways ... ignore your complaint with a smile; make their children sit and be still; or offer you a drink and suggest you join their party. D is acceptable only if you have finished your meal. So why not relax and enjoy another brandy? After all, this is Spain! You can always talk later.

SITUATION 3

You have an appointment with the *notario* (notary public) for 10 am and arrive at his office punctually. The receptionist politely acknowledges your presence and asks you to take a seat. Two hours later you are still sitting there and each time you catch the receptionist's eye, she shrugs her shoulders. Finally she admits that she has no idea when the *notario* will be free. All you need is a signature on a document. You:

A Tell the receptionist you cannot wait any longer and demand that she takes you to the *notario's* private office immediately

B Decide to take matters into your own hands by brushing past the receptionist and storming into his office.

C Beg the receptionist to do her utmost to speed things up as you have another urgent appointment for which you are already late.

D Shout at the poor girl and leave in a huff.

E Leave your document with her and say you will come back for it later.

Comment

As mentioned several times in this book, one of the first things you need to do when you come to live in Spain is adapt to the pace of living. Punctuality is not one of the nation's better developed traits; neither is sticking to appointed times. In this situation the receptionist is clearly incapable of advancing your cause. She may not be there merely for appearance's sake but probably has neither the authority nor the desire to carry out either A or C. B might get you in to see the *notario* who might possibly provide the required signature, but you will probably be told to find another *notario* to act for you in future. E therefore is possibly a better course of action but only if you are prepared to risk losing the document altogether. Perhaps the best solution of all is what the Spaniards themselves do ... the women bring their knitting or the latest romantic novel to while away the waiting hours, and the men may bring a pal for a game of chess!

SITUATION 4

Your husband has been posted to Spain and his company has hired a cleaning woman on your behalf. You have been told that she is reliable and hard-working but that she speaks only Spanish, a language which at present is Double Dutch to you. She is due to arrive on your doorstep shortly and you are wondering how you are going to make her understand what you expect of her. You:

A   Greet her with a smile and take her round the house, pointing and using sign language in the hope that she will understand what you want her to do.

B   Arm yourself with a Spanish phrase book and refer to it frequently whilst you tour the house with her.

C   Ring your husband's office and request that they send someone to act as interpreter.

D Show her where you keep your cleaning aids and let her get on with the work.

E Tell her there's been a mistake as you weren't planning on hiring anyone just yet.

Comment

Definitely not C. Your husband's office may have hired the cleaner on your behalf but that's as far as their involvement in your domestic affairs is likely to be tolerated. If you opt for E because you hope your husband's office will find you another cleaner who can speak a little English, you will not be popular. If you mean to do the housework yourself, you are depriving yourself of the opportunity of having help in the house, giving you more time in which to explore your new surroundings and make new friends. D could lead to problems since the cleaner couldn't possibly know what you expect of her ... Do her duties include washing and ironing, preparing simple meals for your children or merely cleaning? Obviously, it would be far more satisfactory for both of you to have her duties spelled out, and although A might work (more so if you happen to be a talented mime artist), B is clearly the only way to avoid confusion and future misunderstanding.

SITUATION 5

You have been having a lengthy lunch with a group of friends during which the wine flowed like water, the paella was superb and the *carajillos* too delicious to refuse. When the time comes to break up the party, you suddenly realise that you are definitely 'over the limit' as far as the amount of alcohol you have consumed is concerned. You don't have far to go to reach your house and know the road well. You:

A Decide to take the risk and leap in your car, hoping you won't be stopped by the police.

B Try to remember which of your pals was drinking mineral water and ask him for a lift home.

C   Go to the nearest police station and explain your problem, asking for their suggestions.
D   Walk home.

Comment

Walking home is quite a good idea provided you are in a fit state to do so. It should help clear your head! And option B is fine also as long as you can locate such an abstemious pal. A is a no-no. Drink-driving laws in Spain meet European norms and spot checks are quite frequent. C is a possibility but only if you are far from home and none of the other solutions appear to be practical. In the local press, an incident described as *muy valorada* (praise-worthy) by the police featured a man in Benidorm who asked the local police to take care of his car as he feared he was in no condition to drive it. The police looked after his vehicle until the man returned several hours later, had a breath test which proved negative and was able to drive away. The police in fact are very happy to be of assistance as long as the initiative comes from the driver and no offence has been committed, but care should be taken not to abuse their willingness to offer assistance.

189

Their help should only be sought if no alternative solution presents itself.

SITUATION 6

Your next-door neighbour is a dog-lover and has a beautiful pedigree German Shepherd which is left at home all day whilst the owner goes out to work. Bored, the dog takes to paying you a visit and, after a week or so, more or less takes up residence with you even though you have refused to offer it any form of food or drink and have sternly forbidden your children to play with it. After a while you notice that your maid and the postman are unwilling to walk up to your front door without calling you to lock up 'your dog' who by this stage has adopted your house and family as his own, only returning to his owner when the latter comes home at night. His devotion to your family causes him to 'protect' your domain and one day he attacks an intrepid travelling salesman who has dared to wander up to you door. You:

A   Disclaim all responsibility for the attack, insisting that the dog does not belong to you.

B   Offer to take the salesman to the nearest Red Cross station.

C   Offer a sum of money as compensation.

D   Go immediately to the local police station to make a *denuncia* stating that the German Shepherd was trespassing on your property when the attack occurred.

E   Tell the salesman it was all his own fault anyway as he had no business to be knocking on people's doors to try and sell something to them.

Comment

C is to be avoided unless you are prepared to accept responsibility for the dog's attack even though it does not belong to you. D is recommended in addition to any other option as it will protect you should the salesman in turn decide to make a *denuncia* against you, which he has every right to do. The police will then decide what action to take against the owner of the dog.

SPAIN FROM A TO Z

Ancient sites There are numerous archeological sites of great antiquity and extreme interest to historians. Most are 'guarded' to some extent but even so unscrupulous foreigners have been known to infiltrate the areas, removing any 'treasures' they may fancy. This behaviour is reprehensible. There is a 'Treasure Hunting Code' to be followed by those who are interested, and you should make appropriate enquiries before undertaking any such activities.

Baby foods Remember that baby foods are available from pharmacies and supermarkets only.

Currency The Spanish monetary unit is the peseta. Notes are in denominations of 1000, 5000 and 10,000 pesetas and vary in size and colour. Coins are 500, 200, 100, 50, 25, 10, 5 and 1 peseta. As Spain is in the process of changing old coins for new, you may find as many as 16 different coins in circulation at present. The 100 and 500 coins are easily confused, both being gold coloured and almost the same size.

Driving It cannot be too forcefully stressed that most Spaniards believe in the 'survival of the fittest' so be extra careful when you take your car or moped on to the roads. Drivers in Spain seem to be even more unpredictable than elsewhere.

Eyesores To this day, in some parts of Spain, garbage is collected in huge open trucks, and eventually dumped in designated areas where efforts are made to burn it off. Such areas are quite often visible from the main roads, and the stench from the burning rubbish is extremely disagreeable.

Fallas These huge papier mâché effigies can be vulgar and positively crude. The amount of money spent by each community on *fallas* and the fireworks which culminate the village fiestas sometimes causes foreigners to wonder why the government continues to permit such an enormous 'waste'!

Greetings There are appropriate greetings for different times of day and different occasions. Learning them is a good idea.

Hitching Hitching a ride is definitely not recommended, nor is offering rides to strangers.

Informality Not usually to be found amongst the Spaniards, it's the foreigners who prefer informal ways of doing things. So until you are sure that your informality will be appreciated, it's a good idea to stick to 'proper procedures'.

Jams Traffic jams are all too common in many cities and even quite small towns at certain times of the day and during certain seasons. Don't get cross, hot and bothered ... that can only make the jam even more unpleasant to cope with!

Kissing Get used to the idea of being kissed on both cheeks when you are being greeted and on both cheeks when you take your leave. The kisses may not actually land on your cheeks, being merely aimed in your general direction. If there are lots of people involved in greetings and farewells, it can take rather a long time to say hello and goodbye.

Lavatories Most 'rest areas' are equipped with modern and well-kept toilets as well as basins with hot and cold running water. These are also to be found tucked away at the side or back of most petrol stations. Sometimes called *aseos,* the toilets are usually indicated by signs depicting the figure of a woman for 'Ladies' and that of a man for 'Gents'. Occasionally the same doorway leads to both.

Mail delivery This is one of the less efficient services in some parts of Spain due to a lack of sufficient postmen to cope with the ever-increasing numbers of daily deliveries they have to make. Foreigners complain about the length of time it may take for letters to reach them but the blame for such poor service can be laid fairly and squarely at their own doors. The number of postmen employed in an area depends entirely on the number of registered residents in that particular area. As many foreigners prefer not to register, those who do only qualify for enough postmen to deal with their mail. However willing and efficient, the postmen available are often quite incapable of delivering the mountains of mail arriving at the local post office each day!

Newspapers There are numerous Spanish newspapers and magazines such as *El Pais* and *HOLA*. Foreign language newspapers and magazines are easily available in any reasonably-sized town but they are comparatively expensive and usually one or two days late.

Oleanders It is as well to remember that oleanders which are used prolifically as road dividers and hedges, whilst being very pretty when in bloom, are also highly poisonous. You should always wash your hands very thoroughly with soap and water as soon as you have finished fiddling with oleanders.

Postal rates To the United States or Canada, airmail letters cost 69 pesetas up to 15 grams and postcards are 64 pesetas. To the UK and other European Community countries it's 45 pesetas for airmail letters up to 20 grams and the same for postcards. Within Spain letters are 20 pesetas and cards are 18.

Queues Do not exist as such in Spain where *yo primero* (me first) is the rule rather than the exception.

Ramblas Rambling on the Ramblas is one way of spending a pleasant evening. Barcelona's most famous street is a continuous *paseo* for locals and tourists and where you can find 24-hour newspaper kiosks, flower stalls and bird sellers. However, watch out for Spaniards in a hurry who will cut across your path so close in front that you will be hard put to avoid a collision. Should you be unable to avoid a collision, don't expect the Spaniard to apologize! He will turn round and glare at you as if you were at fault rather than the other way round. The Barri Xines (Chinatown), the notorious red-light district, is nearby. The Chinese have long since departed but prostitutes, drug pushers and street thieves could be in evidence so care should be taken if you decide to ramble off the Ramblas!

Stamps These are bought from either the post office or from the state-run *estancos (*tobacconist shops). The latter will normally stock all the fancier issues of stamps to cater to requests for unusual denominations by philatelists.

Tapas *Tapas* (bar snacks) are miniature versions of dishes to be found in restaurants or Spanish homes. They are undoubtedly the most Spanish of culinary traditions. Spaniards love to taste small quantities of lots of different dishes and they will order dishes *para picar* (to nibble at). *Raciones* (larger versions of *tapas*) are popular starters in restaurants.

Unpunctuality Spaniards throughout Spain are notoriously casual about keeping appointments.

Vines Enormous areas of Spain are covered in vineyards and the huge bunches of luscious ripe grapes hanging on the vines at the end of summer are a constant temptation to stop the car, hop out, grab a bunch and sample a few. You will be relieved to know that a Spaniard is unlikely to begrudge you a few grapes 'to sample' on the spot, but filling up a box or basket from the vines to take away with you is another matter. Don't do it unless you are prepared to face an irate farmer! Offering to pay for the grapes might just pacify him.

Water The rain in Spain does not stay mainly in the plain but falls mainly up in the north ... thus the parts of Spain with the poorest soil are the wettest. The rest of Spain is pretty arid and water conservation is an important concern in most areas, particularly on the *costas* where every second house now boasts a swimming pool!

Xenophobia To say that Spaniards suffer from xenophobia would be totally inaccurate. Spaniards do not 'fear foreigners and things foreign' ... quite the opposite in fact! They appear to be trying hard to become just like any other 'European'!

Yawning Yawning and stretching in public is considered very bad manners!

Zebra crossings Treat crossing streets in general with extreme caution and remember that zebra crossings are no guarantee that drivers will give you the 'right of way'.

USEFUL ADDRESSES

GOVERNMENT TOURIST OFFICES
The following Spanish government offices will be able to supply you with information on all aspects of travel to and in Spain:

London
57-59 St James's Street
SW1A 1LD
Tel: 71/499 1169

New York
665, 5th Ave.
NY 10022
Tel: 212/759 8822

Chicago
Water Tower Pl., Suite 915
845 N. Michigan Ave,
IL 60611
Tel: 312/642 1992

Miami
1221 Bricknell Ave.
FL 33131
Tel: 305/358 1992

Los Angeles

8383 Wilshire Blvd, Suite 960
Beverly Hills
CA 90211
Tel: 213/658 7188

CUSTOMS

All enquiries regarding importation of goods which may cause
enquiries to be made by Customs at the Spanish borders should be
addressed to:
Direccion General de Aduanas
Guzman el Bueno 137
Madrid 28040

Sun Alliance Insurance SA
Compania Espania de Seguros
Tuset 20 24
Barcelona 08006

EMBASSIES AND CONSULATES

British and American embassies (in Madrid) and consulates (elsewhere) from whom advice and help can be sought in case of necessity
can be found in the following cities:

Alicante

British Consulate
Calvo Sotelo 1-2
Tel: 96/521 6022

Barcelona

British Consulate
Diagonal 477
Tel: 93/322 2151

American consulate
Via Laietana 33
Tel: 93/319 9550

Balearics
British Consulate
Plaza Mayor 3D
Palma
Tel: 971/71 2445
(Mahon) Tel: 971/36 6439

American consulate
Avenida Jaime III 26
Palma
Tel: 971/72 2660, 72 3600 and 72 5051

Bilbao
British Consulate
Calle Alameda Urquijo 2
Tel: 94/415 7600

American consulate
Avenida Ejercito 11
Tel: 94/435 8300

Madrid
British embassy
Fernando el Santo 16
Tel: 91/308 5201 or 9l/535 5217

American embassy
Serrano 75
Tel: 91/276 3600

Malaga

British consulate
Duquesa de Parcent 3
Tel: 952/21 7571

American consulate
Complejo Sol Playa, Portal 6, Apt 5B
Martinez Gafena
Fuengirola
Tel: 952/47 4891

Seville

British Consulate
Plaza Nueva
Tel: 95/422 8875

American consulate
Paseo de las Delicias 7
Tel: 95/423 1885

EMERGENCIES

Dialling 091 will get you through to the National Police wherever you may be in Spain. Barcelona has an organization called Tourist Attention (Ramblas 43, Tel: 93/301 9060, open 24 hours) which can provide assistance if you've been the victim of a crime, need medical or socio-psychological help or require temporary documents in case originals have been lost. English interpreters are available.

RECREATION
Camping
Federacion Espanola de Empresarios de Camping
Calle Gran Via
88 Grupo 310 8
Madrid 28013

Golf
Real Federacion Espanola de Golf
Calle Captain Haya 9
Madrid

Fishing
ICONA
Avenida Gran Via de San Francisco 35
Madrid

Sailing and Boating
Federacion Espanola de Vela
Calle Juan Vigon 23
Madrid

Diving
Federacion Espanola de Actividades Subacuaticos
Calle Santalo 15
Barcelona

Skiing
Federacion Espanola de Desportes Invierno
Calle Claudio Coello 32
Madrid

BIBLIOGRAPHY

A visit to any lending library in London will provide you with hundreds of titles for books about Spain, in both the following categories. Those listed below are merely ones personally enjoyed and which were found to yield the most useful information. Libraries in other parts of the world are more than likely to be equally rewarding.

GUIDE BOOKS

Fodor's 91 Spain. A very detailed source of information about travelling all over Spain and highly recommended.

A2Z of Settling on Costa Blanca in Spain by Henry Lock. A handy reference for anyone interested in the Costa Blanca in particular.

Blackstone Franks Guide to Living in Spain.

Cooking in Spain by Janet Mendel Searl.

The Food and Wine of Spain and *Tapas* by Penelope Casas. These two books capture the flavour of Spanish life in essays and recipes.

404 Spanish Wines by Frank Snell.

Annuario El Pais. An annual that draws together most aspects of Spanish life. Highly recommended.

Guide to Acquisition of Real Estate in Spain. A leaflet issued by Spanish ministries responsible for Tourism, Consumer Protection and Public Works and available in six languages.

Expatriate Tax and Investment Guide by Allied Dunbar Longman.

International Property Owners News.

Living and Investing in Spain. A pocket guide often available in bookshops.

Living in Spain by Reay-Smith, published by Robert Hale.

Long Stays in Spain by Peter Davey. A complete and practical guide to living and working in Spain.

Lookout Magazine and *Lookout Publications*. Spain's magazines in English and highly recommended.

GENERAL READING

Don Quixote by Miguel Cervantes. A classic.

Blood Wedding by Federico Garcia Lorca. A disturbing book dramatizing the lives of Spain's repressed women.

The Beehive and *The Family of Pascal Duarte* by Camilio Jose Cela. Realistic novels by the 1989 Nobel prize winner for literature.

Spain Delightful essays by Jan Morris.

Spain: A Brief History by Pierre Vilar.

In Spain by Ted Walker. A more vagabond approach to travel.

Spanish Labyrinth by Gerald Brennan.

Homage to Catalonia by George Orwell.

Tales of the Alhambra by Washington Irving.

For Whom the Bell Tolls, *The Sun Also Rises* and *Death in the Afternoon* by Ernest Hemingway. These three novels depict various aspects of Spain – the Civil War, fiesta in Pamplona and bullfighting.

History of Spanish Civil War by Hugh Thomas.

The Spaniards by John Hooper. A must for those interested in discovering how Spaniards have changed since King Juan Carlos came on the throne.

Spain by Sacheverell Sitwell. A little dated but still a wonderful read.

Iberia by James Mitchener. A very thorough and amusing description of travels and reflections.

The Spanish Temper by V.S. Pritchett.

A Stranger in Spain by H.V. Morton.

Two Middle-Aged Ladies in Andalusia by Penelope Chetwode. A very amusing account of adventures on horseback (the second middle-aged lady being the mare La Marquesa).

THE AUTHOR

Born in Singapore of a Belgian father and Russian mother, Marie Louise Graff is well placed to talk about culture shock. Now a British citizen, she spent her school-going years in various parts of the world: Malaysia, New Zealand, Australia and the USA. She has travelled extensively around the world and speaks English, French and some Spanish and Russian.

Marie Louise Graff moved from Singapore to Spain in 1973 upon her husband's retirement. Her family enjoys sailing and is used to warm climates. She is a member of a number of clubs in Spain and likes to drive around Europe with her husband.

Culture Shock! Spain is her first book.

INDEX